See What is Being Said About
Journey-Faith in an Entangled World

"In *Journey-Faith in an Entangled World*, Nancy Sylvester helps her readers to learn how to follow her example of "listening and speaking from a contemplative heart." Through a creative and inviting format, she demonstrates how such practice can open one's mind and spirit to a new and integrative consciousness. *Journey-Faith in an Entangled World* offers wisdom to both new and experienced spiritual seekers, regardless of their faith tradition. This is a Journey I hope to take again and again."

-Margaret Susan Thompson, PhD, professor of history, religion, and women's studies, Syracuse University.

"We need contemplative leaders in this changing era. These leaders must see differently, be able to take a long and very loving look at what our world is birthing, and must possess the capacity to hold it through its labor. Drawing from her rich life as a Catholic Sister, her ministerial leadership, and her decades of contemplative study, practice, and teaching, Sister Nancy Sylvester synthesizes an approach to this time through public contemplation that is both pure gift and quiet challenge. In *Journey-Faith in an Entangled World*, contemplative leaders new and old will find a companion, tutor, and guide, and will want to keep coming back to this text for another level of integration."

-Mary J. Novak, J.D., M.A.P.S., Executive Director, NETWORK Lobby for Catholic Social Justice and Associate of the Congregation of St. Joseph.

"In a time of profound and unsettling change, the pages of *Journey-Faith in an Entangled World* revealed a map of the way I had come, reassurance that I was not lost, a vision forward, practical guidance and tools to move, and the welcome hope of once again joining together in the struggle toward and celebration of Love's evolution. I recommend Nancy Sylvester's book to anyone standing on shaky ground looking for a way forward in faith."

-Leo Lechtenberg, MEd Counseling Psychology, Artist, Missioner to Bolivia, spiritual director St.Vincent DePaul chapter and former Director of Campus Ministry, University of Detroit Mercy.

"Nancy Sylvester's *Journey-Faith in an Entangled World* lifts up the transformative power of the contemplative life. Reflecting on the story of her own transformation in religious life as a Catholic sister, Nancy weaves together insights from mysticism and quantum physics, the natural world and the Christian story. The result points to both the demand and the potential for transformation of consciousness as the next step in humanity's evolution. Engaging in contemplative practice over time helps us awaken to sacred mystery, experience our own transformation, and take up our calling to work for healing and liberation. The times we are living in demand a new way of seeing, with transformational leaders who have the capacity to reimagine our society. Nancy's work is a call to each of us to deepen our contemplative practice, opening ourselves to the power of the divine, transforming us and empowering us, to lead the change our society desperately needs."

-Michelle A. Scheidt, DMin, Senior Program Officer, Fetzer Institute, whose mission is helping build the spiritual foundation for a loving world.

"Imagine a world in which contemplation, deep immersion into the whole of Being, was a regular practice. Nancy Sylvester offers simple techniques and inviting themes for personal and communal reflection. Dialogue that emerges from holding lightly the woes and wonders of the world is a real help and a great hope for cultivating oneness. Just imagine and try it with *Journey-Faith in an Entangled World* as your guidebook."

-Theologian Mary E. Hunt is the Co-director of the Women's Alliance for Theology, Ethics, and Ritual (WATER) in Silver Spring, Maryland, USA.

"To open *Journey-Faith in an Entangled World* is to be drawn into Divine Mystery through the magnetism of contemplation. The journey is urgent and imperative, underlying and suffusing the possibility for personal humanness and the healing and flourishing of our world and planet. As Nancy Sylvester deftly interweaves the unfolding story of contemplation through the centuries with her personal story of contemplation, she invites readers/reflectors to experience this story as our own. In creative spaciousness we are guided toward a center of gravity from which we see who we are and why we are through the lens of infinite love. Transformed by the artistry of contemplation at work in us, we create a living cosmic gallery of justice, peace, and communion. I regard this book as integral to living with meaning in these times. It is an exquisite piece of contemplative art to be entered like an icon forming the seer as a life-long apparition of Love."

-Mary Ann Zollmann, BVM, PhD, Woman Religious, who holds a PhD in spirituality and whose life of ministry in teaching, congregational and national leadership, and spiritual direction has been centered in spirituality.

"Nancy Sylvester, IHM, adeptly captivates what it means to live with purpose and passion in *Journey-Faith in an Entangled World*. Whether delving into the existential or a simple invitation to follow your breath this book invites you to live into the grit of what makes us whole persons in service to mission and creation. She grapples with contemporary challenges through the embodied practice of contemplation. Each section embraces the reader while inviting focused attention through story and reflection. Sylvester is unafraid to enter the scaffolding of human experience while moving to the very center of life as a faith response wholeheartedly loving the world."

-Vicki Wuolle, CSA, PhD, ACC, former Executive Director of the Leadership Collaborative, Co-Creator of Thresholds: Facilitating – Coaching – Consulting.

Journey-Faith in an Entangled World ignites inner excitement and hope for the future. As an addiction nurse and home health care social worker, I truly appreciate the way Nancy Sylvester shares her commitment to contemplation. She offers us ways to experience Divine Love finding ways forward into individual and communal healing. Committed to justice, especially ecological justice, I find her experience of how contemplation transforms us 'to take a long loving look at the real' as we engage with the issues of our day to be extremely helpful. There is no better time to take this journey."

-Sharon McNeil R.N., LMSW, IHM Associate, former ecology director, and founder of the Stronger Together Huddle group whose purpose is to promote the common good in public policy as well as fair and free elections.

Journey–Faith in an *Entangled World*

Nancy Sylvester, IHM

Copyright © 2024 by Nancy Sylvester, IHM

All rights reserved. This book or any portion thereof may not be reproduced in any form or by any electronic or mechanical means, including information storage and retrieval systems, without written permission from the author, except for the use of brief quotations in a book review.

Cover design and illustrations: Rose DeSloover
Digital page design: Judy Olds
Permissions are listed within the Notes section of this book.

Paperback ISBN: 979-8-9911132-0-5
First published in 2024 by the Institute for Communal Contemplation and Dialogue
www.iccdinstitute.com
To request permission email iccdinstitute@aol.com

Printed in the United States of America

Inspiration

Constance FitzGerald, OCD, a friend and mentor, writes that she sees all around us the passion to touch the roots of contemplation often existing as an unrecognized, subterranean force. She wants to bring it above ground into the public forum and to understand its transformative power in our post-modern world.

FitzGerald believes "that only if we are prepared for transformation by contemplation and thereby given a new kind of consciousness and imagination will humanity and the Earth with its various eco-systems survive."[1] She speaks of the importance of becoming educators for public contemplation.

May *Journey-Faith in an Entangled World* help bring this power of contemplation above ground and become part of the education for public contemplation so needed for our future.

Dedication

To all those who in their search for meaning
in this entangled world
are open to both being transformed in Divine Love
and becoming conscious participants
in evolving our future.

Table of Contents

Note from the Author • *xiii*

An Art Exhibit – The Metaphor • *xv*

THE ART EXHIBIT

Gallery One: The Artist's Journey-Faith • 3

• *Journey-Faith in an Entangled World*, Invitation to Transformation • 3

• Spaciousness to Create • 13

Gallery Two: The Medium Needed for Contemplative Creativity • 15

• An Invitation to Transformation • 17

• Contemplation • 21

• Contemplative Practice • 23

• Witnessing Presence • 25

• Contemplative Dialogue • 27

• Communal Contemplation • 33

• Education for Public Contemplation • 35

• Spaciousness to Create • 39

Gallery Three: Seeing the "Real" of Our Times • 41

• A Healthy Planet is the Right to Life • 43

• Embracing the Marias in Our Country • 45

• We Have to be Carefully Taught to Hate • 47

• Learning from the Pandemic • 49

- Clerical Abuse of Children and Women • 53
- Violence Permeating Our Daily Life • 57
- Spaciousness to Create • 59

Gallery Four: Public Life and Democracy • 61
- With Great Diversity, We Are Still One Nation • 63
- Walking a Tightrope to Reinvent Our Democracy • 65
- This Moment Needs Transformational Leaders • 67
- When the Future is Obscure, You Need Radical Trust • 71
- Go Back and Fetch It • 75
- Can Christians Be Progressive? Absolutely! • 79
- Spaciousness to Create • 83

Gallery Five: Christian Feasts • 85
- Advent • 87
- Christmas • 91
- Epiphany • 95
- Lent • 97
- Ash Wednesday • 99
- Triduum • 101
- Holy Thursday • 103
- Good Friday • 105
- Holy Saturday • 107
- Easter • 109
- Spaciousness to Create • 113

Gallery Six: Nature's Inspiration · 115

·Summer · 117

·Fall · 119

·Winter · 121

·Spring · 123

·Spaciousness to Create · 125

Gallery Seven: Transforming Power of Communal Contemplation · 127

·Exercising Contemplative Power · 129

·Living Synodality in a Polarized World · 131

·Consider the Snail · 133

·Cosmic Sentry · 135

·Living Out of Love and Forgiveness · 137

·Evolutionary Hope · 141

·Spaciousness to Create · 145

Notes · 147

Bibliography · 157

Acknowledgments · 175

About the Author · 179

NOTES FROM THE AUTHOR

Welcome to *Journey-Faith in an Entangled World*. Writing a book is a challenging endeavor and the reasons why someone writes a book can be very helpful to deciding whether or not you want to continue reading.

Allow me to share my reasons for writing this book by first posing a few questions.

Do you ever feel that our world is at a chaos point, at the brink, a breaking point, an impasse? Do you sense that much of what was relied upon from the past is no longer working; yet desire to do something about creating the future?

Do you consider yourself a spiritual person and experience a desire for greater meaning in your life but have difficulty discovering it within our post-modern world?

Do you believe in God yet yearn to find ways of expressing your experience of God that reflect your evolving understanding of self, others, and the world?

These are some of the questions that moved me to write this book. I wrote to explore how to address the problems of today from a different consciousness than the one that created them as Einstein so wisely said. I wrote because, for many people across generations, the split between religion and science starting in the 14th century is problematic, alienating, and contributes to the loneliness and polarization we currently experience, and it needs to be addressed. I wrote to understand how I can live authentically within my faith tradition, Catholicism, even as I integrate the insights of evolution, quantum physics, and the development of consciousness within it. I wanted to share how contemplative prayer invited me to 'take a long

> ***Journey-Faith in an Entangled World* is not a book filled with answers. It reflects the contours of the roads I'm traveling into these questions, a journey that is unfinished. If you have had some of these questions, then I hope you will continue reading and join me on this journey.**

loving look at the real' and awakened in me a way of being that involves both transformation of self and re-engagement with the world in ways that could contribute to an emerging future propelled by Love. I wrote to share experiences of God, Divine Mystery, entangled within everyday life as signs of hope on the journey.

Journey-Faith in an Entangled World is not a book filled with answers. It reflects the contours of the roads I'm traveling into these questions, a journey that is unfinished. If you have had some of these questions, then I hope you will continue reading and join me on this journey.

Thank you for opening *Journey-Faith in an Entangled World*. May the words of Christopher Fry's poem, *A Sleep of Prisoners*, guide us on this journey.

The human heart can go the lengths of God ...
Dark and cold we may be, but this
Is no winter now. The frozen misery
Of centuries breaks, cracks, begins to move;
The thunder is the thunder of the floes,
The thaw, the flood, the upstart Spring.

Thank God our time is now when wrong
Comes up to face us everywhere,
Never to leave us till we take
The longest stride of soul we ever took.
Affairs are now soul size.[2]

Nancy Sylvester, IHM

THE METAPHOR OF THE BOOK

An Art Exhibit

As I walk through a museum, I see the artwork as the residue of the artistic process --- the actions of the artist. A finished piece of art holds the time and energy of the artist. It documents sustained interaction --- sustained engagement with a thought, a feeling, a concept, a conclusion.

Rose DeSloover

Art offers sanctuary to everyone willing to open their hearts as well as their eyes.

Nikki Giovanni

The metaphor of an art exhibit organizes this book. As with many art exhibits, you are viewing only one aspect of a very diverse, evolving topic: *Journey-Faith in an Entangled World*. As the quotes above capture, when one views a piece of art one is seeing an expression of the artist's creativity. Creativity is the key process. The process of preparation, of playing with possibilities, of putting paint on canvas or pen to paper is where creative energy flows through and finds expression in various mediums.

Contemplation is the medium used in this exhibit. Through the medium of contemplation, I express my relationship with Divine Mystery. This relationship has evolved over years of practicing contemplation and integrating its wisdom into everyday realities. It transformed the way I see things; it invited me 'to take a long loving look at the real,' a phrase often used to describe contemplation and the contemplative gaze.

You are invited to bring that contemplative gaze to view the art exhibit. The pieces exhibited are not simply

> **Whether contemplation is new to you or part of your own "prayer palette," the invitation through the gallery is to see things anew, 'to take a long loving look at the real,' and to practice this medium. Then give expression to what is emerging in you. At different times throughout the exhibit, you will find a blank 'canvas' for you to do just that.**

reflections to read, pause, and comment on. They are invitations to feel the reality being expressed and to see the inner significance of what is before you. Each person attending an art exhibit is an essential part of creation, taking it in and expressing it in a new way through one's own experience.

Whether contemplation is new to you or part of your own "prayer palette," the invitation through the gallery is to see things anew, 'to take a long loving look at the real,' and to practice this medium. Then give expression to what is emerging in you. At different times throughout the exhibit, you will find a blank 'canvas' for you to do just that.

Galleries One and Two are essential as they orient you to the rest of the galleries. Gallery One takes you on my *Journey-Faith*, sharing the many twists and turns in coming to understand the transformative power of contemplation. Gallery Two reflects on contemplation and its many aspects.

After you exit Gallery Two there is no special order in which to view the rest of the exhibit. Galleries Three through Seven are reflections that I've written over these past years in which I give voice to how I am learning to pray, to see life in new ways, and to engage the world around me as I travel the road of contemplation. Each has a specific focus. Certain ones may immediately attract you or you may want to simply meander through them all, taking as much time as you want or need.[3]

Remember, especially when you see the *Spaciousness to Create* pages, that these are your 'blank canvases' to take time to reflect, enter into contemplation, see what emerges in you, and give expression to your awareness. Consider those pauses as a sanctuary to see in new ways the reality of life.

THE ART EXHIBIT

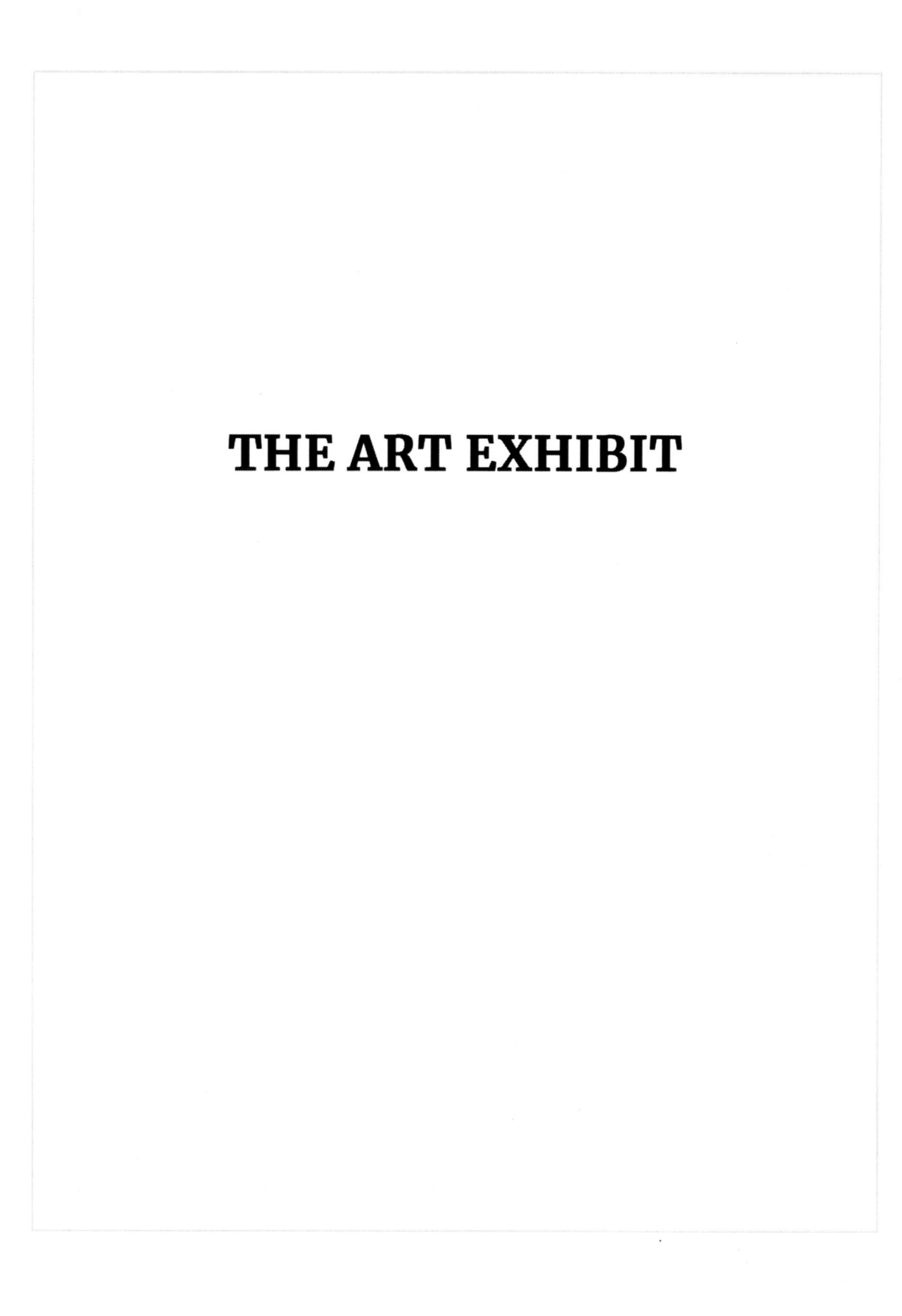

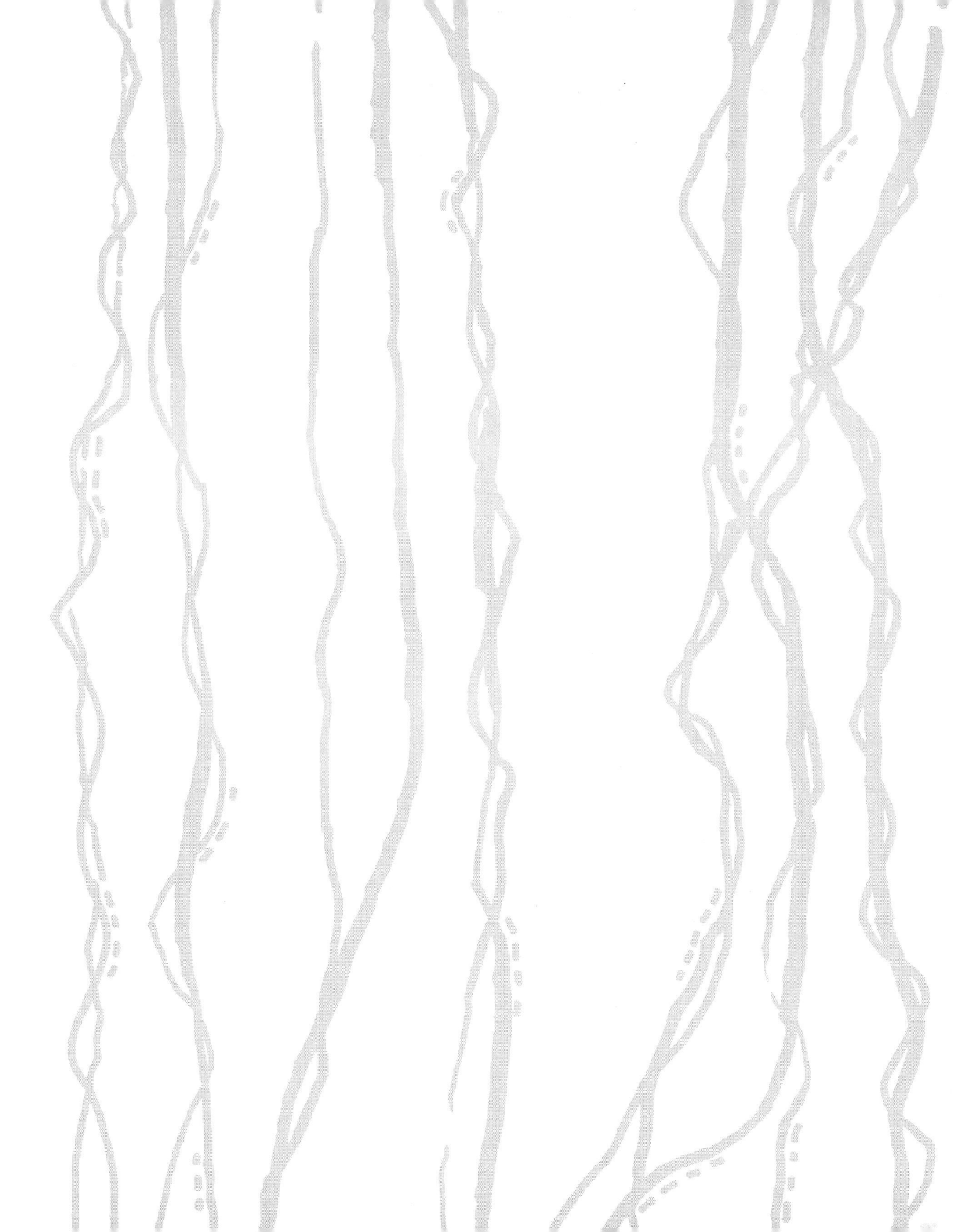

Gallery 1:

THE ARTIST'S JOURNEY

The first gallery is both personal and historical. It is a picture over time of how various experiences in different aspects of life intersect, weave together, and connect to create new understandings of the 'exploration into God' within an entangled world.

Journey-Faith in an Entangled World, Invitation to Transformation

> Ours is not a 'lab faith,' but a 'Journey Faith,'
> a historical faith. God has revealed himself as history,
> not as a compendium of abstract truths.
> Pope Francis[4]

> Journey Faith — a faith that emerges and unfolds on a
> journey, which may have twists and turns, stumbling
> and uncertainty — rather than a 'lab faith'
> in which everything
> is clear cut and neatly defined.
> Robert Ellsberg[5]

When I first read the quotes about *Journey-Faith* I knew that these captured my experience. I grew up with a traditional 'lab faith,' as Robert Ellsberg puts it, for which I am very grateful. However, my life experiences and ongoing education brought into question some of those formulated beliefs. As a professed woman religious, a Catholic sister, this journey was precarious because I had to ask myself multiple times how the God I was experiencing and my faith as it was evolving remained within the Catholic faith tradition.

The term *Journey-Faith* expresses what I am trying to share. It is not a noun, not an object, static and outside of oneself, but closer to a verb ... *Journey-Faith*. It may seem awkward, and one might want to say Journey in Faith or a Faith Journey, but that does not capture it for me. The focus is on both concepts equally: how I experienced the revelation of God in my life and how my life's journey shaped and found expression in Divine Mystery. It is also how the Gospel message of Love evolved in my life and throughout history remaining still relevant for today's challenges.

My *Journey-Faith* takes place in an entangled world. The word entanglement is a key concept in quantum physics. It expresses the inextricable relationship of mind and matter and provides a scientific underpinning for my experience that everything is connected. All of our experiences are interconnected. They weave in and out of each other, creating new insights and understandings. Entanglement embraces the human and divine dimensions of reality. "God and humanity are in an entangled state. The evolution of God and the evolution of humanity cannot be separated."[6] "Matter, mind, person, community, all form the matrix of the living God."[7] It is in such a world that I live my *Journey-Faith*.

People are leaving all forms of organized religion. Often 'lab faith,' a religion's emphasis on doctrinal belief statements, no longer speaks to people's experience of God or supports the emerging spirituality rooted in one's experience. In the absence of a more articulated *Journey-Faith*, many are left spiritually homeless and too often experience a sense of meaninglessness amidst the suffering of our world. I am convinced that part of the alienation, loneliness, depression, and addiction experienced throughout society is due to an absence of believing there is another dimension of reality, beyond the material, which is both transcendent and personal.

I believe those of us who still quest for God in a post-modern world have a responsibility to preach the good news and live out of love in new ways that reflect one's *Journey-Faith*. I believe many of us are on this journey and some of us are uniquely positioned to give voice to this experience. My life has placed me in public positions where I have been invited to write, speak, and teach about this exploration. Now, I sense it is time to step forward and more formally address this experience of *Journey-Faith in an Entangled World*.

To better understand my *Journey-Faith* I need to share some of my history. This is not a memoir. What I hope to do is highlight key moments in my life that embody or illustrate different roads on my journey that intersect and took me in new directions. Each old road leads to a new one and what I am learning becomes entangled with what I know as I continue on my journey navigating the new terrain. The metaphor is not perfect but I found it useful as I hope you do.

Setting Out

I grew up as a very pious and traditional Catholic in a pre-Vatican II Church in Chicago. I loved the prayers and rituals of the Church and had a 'God and me spirituality' that ensured the salvation of my soul. I loved God and wanted to be perfect. Because the Church taught that the highest vocation was that of a vowed religious, I decided to become one. I couldn't wait to wear the religious habit, to choose a religious name, to have time to study and pray, and to live together in community. However, when I arrived in Monroe, Michigan at the Motherhouse of the Sisters, Servants of the Immaculate Heart of Mary (IHM), what I had hoped for and anticipated in terms of religious life was already changing. It was 1966. The Second Vatican Council (1962-1965) had ended and IHMs were already integrating what the Council promulgated.

Today, it is hard to understand what a sea change, seismic shift, or quantum leap Vatican II was for those of us who were Catholic when the Council occurred. And that was especially true for those of us who were canonical religious — or aspiring to be — at that time. For me, the change was symbolized by the decision that our entrance class would not wear the traditional garb of a Postulant and that we would not be changing our names. These were changes that could be seen on the surface but what was happening went much deeper as the Council encouraged a new way of seeing what it meant to be Catholic in the modern world.

Before the Council, Catholicism continued to exist into the 20th century fairly unchanged from the Middle Ages. It retained a monarchical governing structure rejecting a newer form, a more democratic one. It refused to engage with the scientific discoveries of the Enlightenment and the Scientific Revolution of the 17th century. During these years both scientists and philosophers emphasized the superiority of man's capacity to reason as well as the objective nature of reality. As scientific discoveries began to take hold, faith was relegated to the subjective realm of the individual experience. The Church's leaders were being displaced as the major authority in society and people's lives.

This division between science and religion began as early as the 1400s when Copernicus and, later, Galileo explored cosmology, the study of the nature of the Universe. The discovery that the Earth was not the center of the known Universe but rather that the Earth moved around the Sun caused centuries of disavowal by the church. Such a change in cosmology threatened the theology that had been in place over the previous centuries where a three-tier model — an unchanging Earth, Heaven above, and Hell below — was central. This split between religion and science widened and hardened. The cosmology that was in place continued to inform the theology that was officially taught and shaped the doctrine of the Church, its teachings, and its culture. This Traditional vs. Modern approach to the world continued and, for many, continues today.

When Pope John XXIII convened the Second Vatican Council and called all the Cardinals throughout the world together, no one could foresee what would happen. Pope John's famous phrase that "it was time to open the windows and let in the fresh air" was more than fulfilled. The outcome was breathtaking. The sixteen Council documents addressed core issues of Catholic teaching from a new perspective. Some of them were understanding the Church's identity as being involved with the world; studying Scripture from a critical historical context; understanding the primacy of conscience; accepting other faith traditions as paths to God; renewing vowed religious life to its original charisms and seeing it as one of many possible vocations; defending freedom of inquiry in Catholic education; and reclaiming the priesthood of all believers.

Studying these Council documents during formation would significantly influence my *Journey-Faith* as these new teachings became entangled in my life. The other courses we had in Monroe included courses on Vatican II theology and philosophy as well as other classes to complete the first two years of a BA. Complementing our academics, we were learning how to pray and becoming familiar with the mystical tradition and contemporary mystics, Pierre Teilhard de Chardin and Thomas Merton.[8] I completed my degree with majors in philosophy and political science at St. Louis University.

Gaining My Footing

While I was at St. Louis University, I participated in the anti-Vietnam war movement by being a draft counselor and taking part in the boycotts and teach-ins. A very powerful learning during that time was the experience of making a difference by challenging unjust policies. I realized that one could be faithful and loyal to an organization or a church and still question and challenge that which one considers unjust.

During that time, I also taught English in a GED program in a parish adjacent to a low-income housing project. One of the persons I often 'taught' would tell me stories about growing up in the South and how during floods she and her sisters and brothers would float on a mattress to safety. I was with her when she read for the first time. I remember sitting in the quad at the University and wondering why was it that she had just begun to read and I was sitting here studying philosophy. What arose in me with great clarity was that it wasn't because I was better than her or smarter. Rather it was because she was an older, Black woman living in the South and I was a white, younger woman, growing up in the North. I realized then how the various unjust systems operating in our country — policies that shaped housing, education, jobs, health care, etc. — maintained an uneven playing field for so many.

My courses and my experiences were stretching and exciting. I continued to wonder whether, because what I was learning resonated with me, I could stay within the Church. Two events happened — one during the years of formation and the other while I was on my first mission — that continue to be key insights as to how I was able to continue in the Church and on my *Journey-Faith* through the years.

The first was the wisdom of our community's General Superior in responding to a letter I wrote while in the Novitiate — the years learning to be a sister — indicating that I thought I should leave religious life. She suggested that I just take some more time to reflect on whether this way of life was for me. I dutifully obeyed her and realized that I could stay with my questions and concerns and rely on and be supported by the faith of the community.

Throughout my life, I have been privileged and grateful to always have had a larger community of people holding me as I explore, stumble, and integrate my experiences of God with my earlier 'lab faith.' The key and central community has been my IHM Congregation which provided opportunities for ongoing learning, especially in areas of theology and psychology. I also found support within the national Leadership Conference of Women Religious (LCWR), among the countless individual women religious and congregations who traveled a similar path and with whom I have ministered throughout the years. Finally, I am inspired by my IHM sisters, associates, and friends, many of whom no longer can live a 'lab faith' but who live out of love on their own *Journey-Faith*.

The second was a profound experience during a retreat in 1972. I taught Faith in Today's World to Seniors in one of our IHM schools. As I stood before this class of young women and began to speak, I experienced all my words frozen inside a bubble — somewhat like you see in comic books. I was observing myself saying things I no longer believed in. It was startling and I knew I needed to reflect on what it was telling me. I felt I was in a crisis and that I was losing my faith. How could I stay a Catholic sister and not believe? How could I say these words when my mind was trying to make sense of what I had learned in theology and philosophy classes? I knew I couldn't just go on. Fortunately, my congregation was offering directed retreats during Holy Week. Even though I was a first-year teacher, I asked if I could miss three days of class. The IHM principal agreed to let me take the time off to go to the retreat.

During the week I would meet daily with the young priest director. At one point in the retreat, he told me that he felt like I was manipulating him. I was horrified because the one thing I have always tried to be was authentic and not manipulative although I knew I was quite capable of it. But there it was, named by someone who was trying to listen to my spirit.

I left not knowing what to do. Should I pray through the night? Should I fast? All sorts of 'responses' went through me. I decided that none of those were me. Then I awoke early in the morning and walked on the beach of Lake Erie. Alone on this stretch of sand with the sun beginning to awaken, the words of Hosea came to me ... *Yes, I have abandoned you but now I call you back ... you are mine ...* And then I felt these words, *know you have the gift of faith, but for you, the face of God will be ever-changing.* From that experience, I knew not simply intellectually but with my mind, heart, body, and soul that I had the gift of faith and that my understanding of God would always be changing. Being secure in that belief gave me the courage and the confidence to embrace the twists and turns, the stumbling and uncertainty of my *Journey-Faith*.

Becoming Entangled with the World

My 'God and me spirituality' became entangled with the world around me. It continued to be transformed as I began to experience the relationship between living the Gospel — the basis of my faith — and addressing injustice. A statement from the World Synod of Catholic Bishops in 1971 confirmed this belief. They stated that "Action on behalf of justice and participation in the transformation of the world fully appear to us as a constitutive dimension of the preaching of the Gospel."[9]

This connection between the Gospel and action on behalf of justice continued to deepen as I facilitated anti-racism workshops in the 1970s; awakened to a new sense of self through the women's movement as I experienced the systems that oppress women; and rethought Scripture through liberation and other contextual theologies. The work of women theologians greatly influenced and continues to influence my thinking. These include Mary Daly, Elizabeth Schussler Fiorenza, Rosemary Radford Reuther, Elizabeth Johnson, Sandra Schneiders, Ada Maria Isasi-Diaz, Diana Hayes, Mary Hunt, Beatrice Bruteau, Bernadette Roberts, Katie Cannon, Beverly Lanzetta, Joann Conn and Ilia Delio.

Action on behalf of justice became central in my life when I joined the staff of NETWORK, a national Catholic social justice lobby, founded in 1972 by different communities of Catholic Sisters.[10] During these years, 1977-1992, I advocated for just public policies and brought the voices of those adversely affected to Washington, DC to speak to members of Congress. This political ministry afforded me the privilege of meeting people from diverse backgrounds. Extensive travel both within the US and to different countries giving talks and workshops provided me with a great appreciation of our diversity as a global community.

Nurturing My Prayer Life

Throughout my *Journey-Faith*, I have consistently fostered a prayer life which continued to evolve, and which over these last decades has focused primarily on contemplation. Earlier I realized that the formal prayers I had learned growing up no longer expressed how I was experiencing God. As I came to understand how patriarchy operates throughout history and within the Catholic Church, it became impossible for me to relate to a God who was male. For me, words do reflect and reinforce a worldview. Language shapes our capacity to imagine another way of seeing the world, of describing it.[11] Having read mystics in various traditions, I knew there were other ways to pray ... to pray without words. I found the Eastern prayer of contemplation, where you follow your breath to focus your attention and silence your mind, to be very attractive, and I practiced that for many years.

As I continued my contemplative practice, I was attracted to Centering Prayer. Thomas Keating, a Cistercian or Trappist monk, developed this practice which is based on the teachings of the 14th-century spiritual classic, *The Cloud of Unknowing*. Simultaneously, I read and participated in programs that Cynthia Bourgeault offered. Cynthia is a modern-day mystic, an Episcopal priest, a close friend of Thomas Keating, and a master teacher of Centering Prayer.[12]

These last decades I found the work of Constance FitzGerald, OCD, very powerful.[13] She wrote on the transformative power of contemplation within this evolutionary moment. Her writings, together with Bourgeault's integration of Christianity with evolutionary consciousness rooted in Centering Prayer, offered me a way forward in my *Journey-Faith*. Both opened up for me a way of responding to life rooted in Christianity through the practice of contemplation.

Finding and Claiming a Public Voice

These insights significantly influenced the next pathway on my *Journey-Faith*. While I was serving in elected leadership in my congregation, I was elected to the LCWR Presidency and traveled yearly to the Vatican in Rome.[14] It was the visit during my year as LCWR President, that brought home to me in a visceral way, how what I had been learning, praying, and experiencing had significantly changed how I viewed the world and my church.

During that Vatican meeting issues were raised that sadly continue to be with us today if only with the slightest changes: women's ordination, LGBTQIA+ ministry, and the understanding of authority in male religious communities where only ordained priests and not brothers can be in positions of elected leadership.

Surprisingly, it was this last issue that brought me from thinking we had different opinions to knowing we held different world views which kept us at an impasse. Let me try to describe this exchange.

When LCWR went to Rome we went with our male counterparts in the Conference of Major Superiors of Men (CMSM). For years they brought up this issue of a brother's authority within the congregation. CMSM kept requesting that the canon law be changed regarding the prohibition of brothers holding elected office unless all the ordained men were deemed incapable.

When they raised the issue this time, a priest and longtime member of that dicastery, rose up, red in the face, short of stature, and pointing his finger wagged it in front of each of the men and yelled: "Would you want to take orders from a Brother?" With that, every one of the men, which included brothers and priests, said a resounding YES.

Perhaps it was because as women religious we had been back and forth with the Vatican about the issues of ordination and gay/lesbian ministry, but this issue made transparent to me a clearer line of separation. The Vatican believed that one's authority came from ordination and not from baptism. If they could not accept a brother to exercise authority within his own congregation, how would they ever accept a woman?

What became clear to me was that there was one Church that continued the monarchial clerical system and all that accompanies that, and another that had begun to live out of the priesthood of believers integrating the insights of the past 300 years within the faith. We didn't just hold different opinions, we held different worldviews. Our consciousness about who we are and what we are about as Church has developed differently.

This trip to Rome shaped my LCWR Presidential address in 2000 where I spoke about how women religious were at an impasse with some in the official Church.[15] Inspired by FitzGerald's article, "Impasse and Dark Night," I told the close to 1,000 sisters assembled that we need to bring this reality of impasse to contemplation and to stay in contemplation long enough to see with our hearts how we can respond; then enter into a communal contemplative space to engage together as to how to move forward.[16]

I knew that most of the ways we responded to the Church and the social justice issues of the day, no longer worked. I believed we had to imagine new possibilities from the very core of our being, from the place where we encounter Divine Mystery. It had to come from contemplation.

This realization called forth in me the decision to start the Institute for Communal Contemplation and Dialogue (ICCD) in 2002.[17] The contemplative experience offered another way of entering the breakdown of societal structures and dominant worldviews, of engaging impasse. The nature and urgency of our global situation called us beyond individual contemplation to engage the impasse through communal contemplation. Together we needed to create the time and space to enter into conversation in a way that opens us up to hear and be changed by each other. Dialogue seemed the appropriate form of discourse to engage with others from a contemplative stance. I felt that engaging in communal contemplation can create possibilities that could affect the transformation of not only self but societal structures as well.

Learning to Understand

This belief that communal contemplation is transformative for both the individual and the larger world became stronger in me as I read extensively about the new science, the new Universe story, systems theory, integral theory, spiral dynamics, quantum physics, and evolutionary thought. Many of these authors saw connections between faith and the emerging scientific thinking of our time.[18]

The insights of Charles Darwin, Thomas Berry, and Brian Swimme struck awe in me as I began to understand the creation story through the lens of evolution, the new universe story, and realized that through time we have all evolved from the original flaring forth.[19] Life emerged from single cells to complex organisms, differentiating and diversifying toward higher levels of material complexity and consciousness until mammals and humans emerged. We live in an interconnected web of life. We are all one. We do not live in isolation;

rather what happens in one part of the world affects other parts of our planet as the climate crisis is showing us. What we do matters. Realizing that the next stage of evolution is seen as an evolution of human consciousness confirmed my belief that those of us rooted in the Gospel message of love have a responsibility to help shape that emergence.

I saw a connection between the evolution of human consciousness and the work of Ken Wilber and Don Beck.[20] In particular, the theory of Spiral Dynamics Integral (SDi) offered me a framework to explain the evolutionary development of consciousness collectively and to understand one's own stage of consciousness.[21] This theory shows how human consciousness beginning with the earliest humans is shaped by value systems and life conditions. It describes stages that like a spiral beginning from the same source continue to move up and out, always circling back but on a slightly different trajectory. With each new turn, there are different life conditions and more diverse beliefs, values, and behaviors. Each succeeding stage, while diversifying, ideally includes the wisdom of previous stages. At whatever stage an individual, nation, or culture is in, what one believes about reality is the 'one right way.' Around eighty years ago a newly emerging stage was documented that seemed to make a significant shift from these earlier stages. With this new stage, there is a greater capacity to embrace complexity, paradox, diversity, and a more non-dual or spectrum way of thinking. One no longer sees everything as separate but rather perceives the wholeness of reality and its interconnected parts. At this stage, one does not believe their view of reality is the only right one but sees the partial truths in all the stages, in all polarities, and integrates the healthy values of every stage. The skills and behaviors developed at this stage deepen one's capacity for dialogue and for discovering new ways of addressing the volatile issues of our time. This emerging stage of consciousness is called integral consciousness.

When I read Paul Levy's work, *Quantum Revelation*, the connection between the emerging stage of integral consciousness and the insights of quantum physics became clearer. Levy writes "Quantum physics is introducing us to a radically new way of seeing, conceptualizing, and understanding that profoundly impacts human thinking, feeling, sensing, knowing, and being. As if the universe itself were giving us a cosmic physics lesson, what quantum physics is revealing to us requires a completely new way of picturing and thinking about the universe, our place in it, as well as who we are."[22] This seemed to echo SDi's theory that the next emerging stage of integral consciousness is a quantum leap in evolutionary development.

I saw a connection between what this emerging integral consciousness is asking of us from the perspective of the sciences and what is asked of us in the radical transformation of self through the dark night of the soul described by the mystics.

As one deepens contemplative practice, obstacles are encountered that prevent us from becoming our authentic selves, the selves that are Imago Dei. Through the ongoing conversion process of contemplation, we face into those worldviews, values, and behaviors that have shaped us, too often blinding and controlling our ability to respond to the injustices of our time. We are blinded by our own beliefs and worldview that the way we see something is the only right way. As we begin to surrender to Divine Love we begin to live into Christ consciousness, learning how to respond to the world around us out of love with great compassion and not primarily fear.

For me, entering into this process of self-transformation, I became more aware of my growing capacity for ambiguity, paradox, and complexity. The possibility is there to see the wholeness of each other and our potentiality, even though I often fail. I sense I can hold more spaciously every 'right answer' so that together we might explore and imagine new possibilities for the future.

And Now...

Where I am on the journey now convinces me that the polarized world within which we live is challenging us to accept our responsibility to become our authentic selves through contemplation as we contribute to the emergence of an integral consciousness.[23]

My *Journey-Faith* is still evolving. Formed in the Catholic faith, rooted in the Gospel of Jesus, entangled with the post-Vatican II theologies, experiences of injustice, insights of science, cosmology, and psychology, and committed to the contemplative journey, I've come to see things differently. For me, it is a both/and world. It is faith with its multiple traditions together with the sciences exploring the God quest. It is the social justice movements that call us forward in new ways and invite a strengthening of Gospel values. It is faith in our capacity to enter into Christ consciousness and respond to the world out of love. It is believing contemplation with its deepening interiority is transformative, supporting an upward/outward movement toward greater inclusivity, compassion, peace, justice, and love for the planetary community.

The reflections that make up this 'art exhibit' are my attempts to integrate my *Journey-Faith* with the realities of life. What I believe transforms how I 'see' the injustices of our time, the leadership we need in our political life, the Christian liturgical feasts, the seasons, and the future. They are incomplete utterances which I'm sure will evolve.

I am still on my *Journey-Faith*, really only a beginner. I believe that as each of us experience our own *Journey-Faith*, we are contributing to the reawakening of Christianity and other religious impulses in our emerging global community. It invites us to a new way of knowing and being. Karl Rahner, SJ, a renowned German theologian, captures it best when he said:

> *The Christian of the future will be a mystic, having had an experience of God or s/he will be nothing at all.*[24]

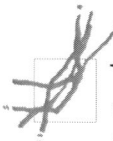

SPACIOUSNESS TO CREATE

Take time to breathe and enter the spaciousness of your heart.
What is rising within you about your Journey-Faith?
Bring expression to it creatively through words, drawing, poetry, doodle, or ...

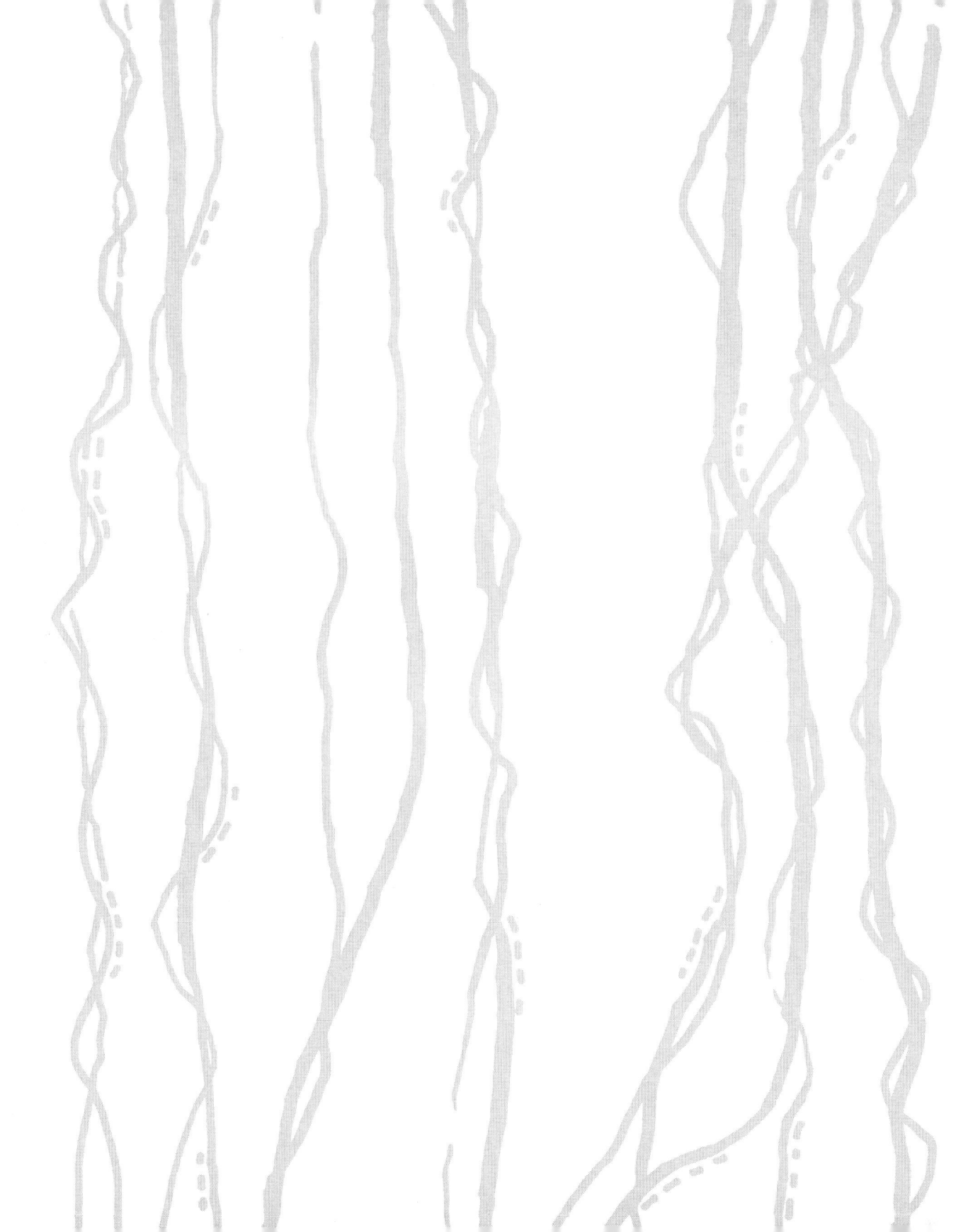

Gallery 2:

THE MEDIUM NEEDED FOR CONTEMPLATIVE CREATIVITY

The medium with which art is expressed varies. In this exhibit the essential medium is contemplation. Whether contemplation is new to you or part of your own 'prayer palette,' the invitation throughout the gallery is to see things anew, 'to take a long loving look at the real.' As you enter Gallery Two, you are invited to reflect on different aspects of contemplation and contemplative practice and then to practice this medium giving expression to what is emerging in you. These materials are offered to you for your use throughout the rest of the exhibit to enhance how you see the pieces and invite you into a new way of seeing.[25]

- **An Invitation to Transformation**

- **Contemplation**

- **Contemplative Practice**

- **Witnessing Presence**

- **Contemplative Dialogue**

- **Communal Contemplation**

- **Education for Public Contemplation**

• An Invitation to Transformation

'To take a long loving look at the real' is a way of describing contemplation. I have always found that description very captivating. Our consciousness, the values, beliefs, and worldviews through which we see reality, is often like the air we breathe, taken for granted and not often in our awareness. When we encounter something new and different, someone or something that doesn't fit into our preconceived ideas, belief system, or worldview, there is a tendency to deny it, to close our eyes to this possibility. We can stop there and resist any change in current perception. Or we can begin to explore what is behind and underneath the words, the actions, and/or the demands. What can emerge is an understanding that reveals that this is a call for a new way of seeing, calling us 'to take that long, loving look at the real.'

I found myself reflecting on how, over the years, the horizons of my seeing have been stretched and deepened as my experiences make me aware of my consciousness and invite a shift in how I view reality.

I thought about when I became aware of the women's movement and how my eyes were opened to see the inequality of women within political, ecclesial, and familial arenas. Language, cultural stereotypes, policies, and structures shaped the way I thought about who women were; what we could aspire to; and how we usually tolerated abusive behaviors.

Another area that opened up a new way of seeing for me was the cry of those who have been written out of a history that is predominantly a narrative written from the white, straight, male, Christian perspective. It is perhaps only now — even though this reality has existed for centuries — that more of us can "see" or realize history in different ways.

For those of us who are being asked to see our biases

Transformative Power of Contemplation, a new way of seeing, a new way to pray, a new way to respond.

Spiral Dynamics Integral deepens my understanding of the transformative power of contemplation creating a flow that mutually enhances each other.

rooted in privilege — race or class or gender or sexual orientation — it isn't easy. At first, it might not even make sense to us. Then, with awareness of what was happening, we began to make this new piece of knowledge part of the whole of how we talk about who we are as a people, as a nation, and as a planetary community.

I am realizing more and more that the capacity to see things in new ways and the openness to try to understand those who are different or the viewpoints that challenge my current beliefs doesn't just happen. For me, it is through an openness to expand my worldview and my contemplative practice that a capacity develops in me to see anew. I am more aware of what is going on in my life and in the world. I am more open to see in new ways what I have taken for granted and assumed was the only and correct way to view things.

Beatrice Bruteau explains why this shift in consciousness is difficult:

> ... my approach is to consider that human behavior takes place in a net of interactions and interconnected ideas, feelings, attitudes, and unacknowledged assumptions, which I call a 'consciousness-net.' This consciousness-net is a worldview, the basic human artifact.... It is the background for everything else that we think or feel or do. Only insofar as something falls within the assumptions of this worldview can it be perceived, noticed, and responded to.... We presume without any question arising, that our basic way of perceiving the world is the way the world really is.[26]

The insights into how consciousness has evolved through time are also helpful to understanding why it is a challenge to shift our worldview. In the theory of Spiral Dynamics Integral (SDi), humankind has evolved through six stages of consciousness based on different life conditions and value systems. This helps us understand why people think in different ways about virtually everything. People, at whatever stage they are at, believe that how they see the world is the right way. This is beginning to change as new stages are emerging that seem to make a leap from the previous ones. Persons at this new 'integral' stage of consciousness are comfortable with complexity and a new way of seeing the whole. They see the partial truths of all the polarities that are part of our lives and integrate the healthy values of every stage to resolve conflicts and create new, emerging possibilities for peace and well-being in an evolving world.

Both the theory of Spiral Dynamics Integral (SDi) and understanding of human consciousness deepen my understanding of the transformative power of contemplation.[27] Together they create a flow that mutually enhances each other. Contemplation continues to deepen my interior journey where I become aware of my shadow, biases, assumptions, and worldviews. These shape both how I 'see' the world around me and how I 'react' to all that is going on. The evolution of consciousness helps me understand the various stages that operate within me and how I've been influenced by multiple factors of family, race, culture, and religion, to name a few. That heightened understanding is now part of who I am when I engage in my contemplative practice.

The ongoing contemplative journey inward invites me to a greater letting go, or kenosis, as I become more my authentic self. Being more aware of what limits my vision, I open myself to the greater complexity and diversity of alternate worldviews. This response finds outward expression in the values, beliefs, and wisdom of the next emerging stage of human consciousness or integral consciousness.

For me, the transformation of consciousness and the transformative power of contemplation, opening the spaciousness to see in new ways, create the capacity to contribute to the transformation of the world.

• Contemplation

Prayer can take many forms. There are the formulated prayers that we use throughout our lives. Being in and with nature is another common way that many of us begin to experience the presence of the Divine. The use of our imagination in picturing ourselves in a Gospel story leads many of us deeper into encountering Jesus. "Lectio Divina" addresses Scripture as the living Word of God and is a practice of scriptural reading, meditation, and contemplation intended to promote communion with God. Walking meditation teaches us "mindfulness," another way of becoming still and present. Poetry, art, and dance can move us to a different state of consciousness as well.

Contemplation is a form of prayer that invites us to drop down into spacious silence to encounter God, Divine Mystery, within us and to rest in unconditional Divine love. We do not have to think or imagine. We just try to be still. In doing so we learn to withdraw attention from our thoughts to rest in a gentle open attentiveness to divine reality itself. This kind of prayer is known as a non-discursive form of prayer.[28]

This type of non-discursive form of prayer is found in both the Eastern and Western faith traditions. Both traditions employ a way to still your mind and enter a spaciousness within, where you encounter Divine Love.

Paradoxical as it is, in entering the spacious silence to which contemplative practice invites us, we awaken to all that is going on in life, without grasping, clinging, or internalizing. We consent to the workings of God, Divine Mystery, within us.

Over time through contemplative practice, our hearts are being opened to do the difficult work of facing into our shadow, our assumptions, and our biases. We recognize the righteousness that comes from 'my one right way' of looking at things; we are in touch with what triggers our reactions to people and issues and the reasons why.

> *Contemplation ... invites us to drop down into spacious silence to encounter God, Divine Mystery, within us ...*
>
> *Through contemplation we consent to our transformation. We become our authentic self.*

We begin to perceive reality in a new way. Our consciousness moves beyond the either/or, win/lose, dualistic way of knowing into a greater sense of the whole. This non-dual consciousness sees first an interconnectedness, within which there is differentiation.

Our hearts are being transformed. Seeing with a contemplative heart, we acknowledge we are both victim and perpetrator, oppressed and oppressor. Our hearts awaken with compassion, opening to the possibility of forgiveness and reconciliation.

We are strengthening the capacity of understanding another's values and being willing to explore with others new possibilities. This frees us to passionately respond and advocate around specific issues while authentically respecting and loving the people with whom we disagree.

Through contemplation, we rest in the unconditional love of Divine Mystery and consent to our transformation. We become our authentic self, putting on the mind of Christ.

• Contemplative Practice

It takes time for most of us to drop down into spacious silence and encounter Divine Mystery working within us, awakening us to who we truly are and where we are aligned with Divine Love. That is why we speak of contemplative practice. It takes time to become more spacious, more attentive, and more awake. You probably won't feel anything initially during your contemplative practice, but, over time, you experience transformation as your being and your very way of seeing shifts, and you come closer to putting on the mind of Christ. You begin to respond to situations from the place of Witnessing Presence.

Although contemplation and mysticism have been part of Western Christianity from its beginnings, it became primarily associated with cloistered religious from the Middle Ages onward. In the 1970s, John Main, OSB, introduced a way of contemplative prayer using a mantra or short prayer phrase. One would say part of the mantra on the in-breath and another part on the out-breath such as 'Mara-natha,' 'Jesus-Mercy,' etc. The purpose of repeating the mantra in conjunction with our breath was to bring our minds to a focal point of attention. Both were ways to bring us into the presence of Divine Mystery dwelling within us.

Around the same time, Thomas Keating, OCSO, retrieved for Western Christianity a practice based on the classic mystical text, *The Cloud of Unknowing,* that he called Centering Prayer. This form of contemplative practice focuses more on "intention" than on attention. There is still a word or phrase involved, but in this case, it is a sacred word you choose or which chooses you. As you begin your sitting practice you pray this word gently and then let it go. You consent to the workings of Divine Mystery within you for your transformation and that of the world.

This contemplative prayer is one of release. You gently say this word when you become distracted which is normal

> *Choose a sacred word.*
> *Gently pray that word.*
> *Let it go.*
> *Consent to the workings of Divine Mystery within you.*
>
> *Over time, you experience transformation as your being and your very way of seeing shifts.*

and natural. This can be a thought, an emotion, a concern, or a physical discomfort. By returning to the word you release your grip on what you would usually pay attention to and open yourself to Divine Mystery working within you.

     It is a dropping down into that spaciousness you are creating within yourself, signifying a willingness to release old patterns of thinking and action compassionately without judgment. This process becomes the material for our transformation. This pattern of surrender, attention, and compassion is like the kenosis of Jesus, whose self-emptying love formed the core of his own self-understanding and life practice. It is one path of spiritual transformation.[29]

<u>Now you are ready to begin contemplative practice:</u>

1. Choose which practice you will follow — following your breath with or without a mantra; or saying your word and then letting it go.

2. Find a quiet and uncluttered space. You may want to have a candle and, or object of beauty in your space. Get comfortable in the chair, on the cushion or wherever you have chosen for the sitting. Sit as straight as you can. Remember your body is a conduit for your breath, for the flow of your energy, and is a support for the practice and not a distraction. Bring a timer or clock which you can set for a period of time.

3. Then take a minute or two to settle in. Become aware of the ground upon which you sit. Feel it in your feet. Sense the energy surrounding you. You might want to do a quick body scan to see where there is tightness or where you feel discomfort. Pause and simply bring your attention to it, breathe into it, and then release. Take a few deep breaths relaxing your shoulders and neck. Find a space a few feet in front of you where your eyes can focus and a place for your hands.

If it helps you might want to visually picture yourself taking those things that are on your mind — the chores, jobs, family, worries, shoulds, woulds, and coulds — and putting them in a backpack and placing them outside your space until you are finished.

4. Breathe deeply a couple of times. Set the intention to be open to the workings of Divine Love within you for your transformation and for the transformation of the world.

5. Begin following your breath, saying your mantra or speaking your word.
When you are distracted — it is not if but when — simply return to the breath, mantra, or word. Remember, a distraction is anything that starts your mind going — a thought, an image, a feeling, an itch, an agenda item for your next meeting. Simply let go without judgment and return to your practice creating that spaciousness within where transformation happens.

6. Do this practice for 20 minutes, preferably twice a day.

• Witnessing Presence

When you begin your contemplative practice, it is not unusual for you to wonder if anything is happening. You don't hear voices or have visions. You don't necessarily feel anything. You wonder where is this transformation that is talked about?

It comes over time. As you continue your contemplative practice of surrender, attention, and compassion, your way of seeing and being is radically transformed.

As you deepen the spaciousness in which you surrender to Divine Loving you awaken to your authentic self, your true self, your Christ consciousness. In this process, new neurological pathways are being laid down for transforming love and relationality. This awakening can become the source and support of a new stage of integral consciousness that embraces ever increasing inclusivity, interrelatedness, cooperation, and co-creation with others and the world.

This inner movement, in opening us to Christ Consciousness, transforms our inner spiritual self. It frees us to observe, respond, and participate in the world from love rather than fear or blame. That is the place of Witnessing Presence. It is a presence carried in the knowing heart that, like a magnet, pulls us toward our center amid everything that is happening.

It is from this center that we can see the Christ Consciousness in each person. We can see their underlying wholeness and infinite potential. It is only then that we can reach out in dialogue and true service.[30]

It is from these latter and more conscious parts of the self, from Witnessing Presence, that we want to respond to the breaking of the "frozen miseries of centuries." It is from this space that we can engage differences making free choices as to how we want to be in moments of extreme polarization and crisis.

> *As you deepen the spaciousness within and surrender to Divine Loving, new neurological pathways are being laid down for transforming love and relationality.*
>
> *Observe, respond, and participate in the world from love rather than fear or blame.*

How does this authentic/true self become more visible to us?

Like a glacier, we think we know who we are but this is only the tip of the iceberg. We must awaken to our own experience and begin to reflect on it so we can detach from it. Thomas Keating offers a way to do this in his work on the psychology of Centering Prayer which he calls Divine Therapy, which I am drawing on for this section.[31] There are three energy centers we are born with: the need for security and survival; the need for affection and esteem; and the need for power and control. These very natural needs are never fully satisfied because of perceived or real deprivations. However, as we enter the age of reason we use our rational faculties to justify, glorify, and rationalize our behavior. We develop a set of protective behaviors driven by a sense of need and lack. Thomas Keating calls this the false self that, in action, represses or inappropriately expresses the feelings generated when our energy centers are frustrated. He calls these first three energy centers 'our programs for happiness, which can't possibly work.'

It is this false self, identified with this desire for happiness in ways that cannot possibly work, that we must detach from. Keating teaches that contemplative prayer is a direct catalyst to this process of purification and the healing of the unconscious. As we sit in centering prayer with the intent to rest in and trust in God, the unconscious begins to unload 'the emotional junk of a lifetime.' This requires courage and inner presence to sustain the pull of our woundedness and self-justification. Keating believes that contemplative prayer over time helps us to confront our unconscious motivations creating the necessary depositions for a relationship with God.

The behaviors that are motivated by these early needs and desires are deeply rooted in us and will rise up when they are seemingly threatened by change, by whatever is felt to be the "thaw, the floods, the upstart Spring." It is only as we wake up and begin this self-inquiry that we can embrace a new stage of consciousness.

As we detach from those impossible programs for happiness, we find ourselves responding from the place of Witnessing Presence. We participate in the world out of love rather than from fear or blame. We are growing in our capacity to respond from our authentic and true selves, from Christ consciousness, and with enormous compassion.

This growth process lasts a lifetime. Just as we become aware of how we want to respond, and often do so out of love, it isn't unusual to return to old ways of responding to situations. Don't become discouraged. It is simply that those 'false programs for happiness' are deeply embedded in our evolutionary past. Contemplation invites us to keep going ... going deeper. We are changing and our transformation continues always integrating our newest insights and behaviors as we continue dropping ever deeper into Divine Loving and our ongoing transformation.

• Contemplative Dialogue

Through contemplative practice we become more aware of our experience — more self-reflective — more awake — we desire to be and act differently so as to respond to situations from this deeper place. We want to respond — to listen and speak and act sourced from our contemplative heart. We want to embody Christ Consciousness.

Our old ways of being and acting don't seem to fit — our old identity doesn't seem to fit. We are being invited to more fully embrace our authentic self. It is the place where being and doing are one.

We are moving from a binary consciousness, a more 'me' centered one, to a non-dual one, a more 'other' centered compassionate focus. We are carving new neural pathways in our brain. As with an upgrade in our computer system, there are significant changes in how we think about things and in how we behave to express these new insights. We must learn how to listen and speak from a contemplative heart.

Listening and speaking from a contemplative heart is key to engaging with others in dialogue. Dialogue is far richer than debate, advocacy, an exchange of ideas, negotiation, or discussion. It is not a one-sided winner-take-all approach to issues. Rather, it is to begin to think together. Engaging in dialogue means that you are willing to look at all the assumptions including your fundamental beliefs and worldviews if necessary.

For many of us, this kind of listening and talking together demands new behaviors and skills. David Bohm, the physicist, wrote extensively on "dialogue." He saw that dialogue explores the manner in which thought is generated and sustained on a collective level. He saw this manner of inquiry as probing the critical questions of

> *We must learn how to listen and speak from a contemplative heart.*
>
> *The skills of dialogue when sourced from a contemplative heart help us with our work of transformation.*

identity, culture, and meaning. For Bohm dialogue was an invitation to collectively explore the prospect of an enhanced humanity. [32]

Dialogue invites us to probe our assumptions, to keep peeling away the layers of inference and bias. To do this successfully one's ego cannot be in control. Dialogue invites us to be part of a larger community of meaning. It is an opportunity to create a new consciousness, new understandings. The skills of dialogue when sourced from a contemplative heart help us with our work of transformation.

When the Institute for Communal Contemplation and Dialogue (ICCD) began, the first program was *Engaging Impasse: Circles of Contemplation and Dialogue*. Jean Alvarez, social psychologist, process facilitator, and teacher of dialogue, was part of the planning committee for the overall creation of the Institute, a member of the design committee, and one of the guides for each of the three sessions of the Engaging Impasse program. A critical component of the program was learning and practicing the skills of dialogue. Jean wrote an excellent synthesis of key writers in the field of dialogue which was used in that program and continues to be used to teach people these critical skills. I have drawn on her articulation over the years. I have not found anything better than her article, "Dialogue and Mom's Hash." The section that follows is hers although you will have to go to the website to find the recipe for her Mom's Hash:[33]

Dialogue and Mom's Hash

As we have tried to sort out what structures and mindsets would make it most possible for participants to find their way to this kind of conversation, we have come to focus on three sources: Parker Palmer, an educator who writes from the perspective of the Quaker tradition; Pema Chodron, who teaches from the perspective of the Buddhist tradition; and Bill Isaacs, who writes from an organizational perspective informed by physicists and philosophers.

Parker Palmer

In his 1993 book, *To Know as We Are Known: Education as a Spiritual Journey*, Palmer writes of the three characteristics essential to creating a space for learning: Openness, Boundaries, and Hospitality. Because dialogue is, at its heart, a process for deep learning, Palmer's suggestions resonate with our experiences of dialogue.

To create openness means "to remove the impediments to learning that we find ... within us, to set aside the barriers behind which we hide so that truth cannot seek us out. We not only 'find' these obstacles around and within us; we often create them ourselves to evade the challenge of truth and transformation.... If we are to open space for knowing, we must be alert to our fear of not knowing and to our fearful tendency to fill the learning space. First, we must see that not knowing is simply the first step toward truth.... Second, we must remember that we not only seek truth but truth seeks us as well. When we become obsessed with our own seeking, we fill the space with methods and hypotheses and reports that may be mere diversions. But when we understand that truth is constantly seeking us, we have reason to open a space in which truth might seek us out."

Boundaries help us to abide in the open space that we have created. We frequently think of boundaries as things that keep other people, things, or events out of our space, but Parker Palmer uses the word to remind us of our inclination to flee from pain, uncertainty, and not-knowing. Faced with the open space necessary for dialogue, we must notice and challenge our desire to flee into memories, tangential thoughts, comparisons: anything that protects us from the anxiety of unknowing. As a meditator acknowledges and moves beyond the chattering of "monkey mind" by quietly saying "thinking" and then emptying the mind again, so the person engaged in dialogue notes each time she escapes beyond the boundaries of the conversation, and gently calls herself back to the uncertain but fertile open space.

In the open space we have created, feelings of anxiety, uncertainty, and discomfort with not-knowing easily arise. The antidote to these feelings, Parker Palmer suggests, is to bring an attitude of hospitality. By hospitality, he means a sense of welcome that makes it possible for each participant to enter the space certain that her ideas — however tentative — are valued, her struggles are a source of richness to the group. Hospitality does not imply a lack of rigor or a culture of unquestioning agreement with all ideas, but rather a wholehearted invitation to each idea and to all explorations-including critiques-of those ideas.

Pema Chodron

The particular practice for which Pema Chodron is best known is tonglen, the practice of intentionally breathing in those things we find painful and want to resist, and breathing out those things that bring us pleasure and that we want to hold on to. Three words that she uses frequently to describe the self-preparation for this practice are *softness, spaciousness* and *welcome*. Unlike Parker Palmer's three words, these do not refer to three different qualities, but are just different ways of imaging the same experience: that of opening to receive what we would like to keep at a distance, or holding lightly what we would like to keep forever.

In dialogue, where there is an assumption that differences are important manifestations of a reality more complex than any individual is able to perceive alone, and therefore an intent to explore the unique perspectives of each participant, this quality of softness, spaciousness or welcome is an important one to cultivate. It enables us to hold our own understandings lightly, offering them to the group without demanding that they remain unchanged. And it enables us to make space within ourselves to receive the perspectives of others, without the hard shell of resistance that so frequently causes us to reject a new or different idea without truly exploring it.

Bill Isaacs

Bill Isaacs' writing on dialogue is — we think — the most comprehensive that can be found. It includes the conceptual grounding for the practice (primarily from the physicist David Bohm), connections to philosophers and others whose thinking relates to dialogue, a description of the stages often experienced in a dialogue, and suggestions for attitudes and skills that enable one to be a contributing participant.

We add three ingredients drawn from Isaacs to our recipe for successful dialogue. All three are simple, but surprisingly challenging.

First, the pace of the conversation is quite slow. Accustomed as we are to beginning our response just as or just before the previous speaker has finished (which means that we decide what we want to say long before that person has finished), we find the measured pace of dialogue a real challenge. Isaacs' assumption is that we need to listen to all of the previous idea before we respond, letting that idea in its fullness find its way into the soft and receptive space we have created in ourselves. Only then do we know whether we really have something to say in response. Isaacs encourages us to "let the sound [of the previous speaker's words] cascade," in the same way that we can let the sound of a Tibetan singing bowl resonate, hearing the different qualities of its sound as it fades slowly into silence. The richness of another's thinking is often revealed in the attentive silence that follows the words, much more than in the quick hunch that arises mid-sentence or mid-paragraph in the mind of the listener.

Second, it is important for each participant to set aside our usual mindsets of evaluation and critique, and bring first an attitude of curiosity. It is curiosity that endows the silence in dialogue with the potential for new insights or understandings of complex truths. Without curiosity, the silence simply becomes an opportunity for the listener to gather more incisive critiques, better-developed arguments. Some of the questions we ask ourselves in the silence...

   1. (If we find ourselves immediately disagreeing) "How might this be making

sense to the speaker? How is my own mental model being challenged by what the speaker is saying?" (This question reminds us that while what we think always feels like truth to us, it is in fact only a mental model: a set of images, stories and assumptions that we have woven together to help us make sense of a complex reality.)

2. "Am I feeling any mental/emotional discomfort or unrest? If so, what is evoking that reaction in me?"

3. "Am I feeling a sense of urgency to respond to the speaker? What, in me, is the source of that urgency? Why is it hard for me to let these ideas go 'uncorrected'?"

4. "How often have I heard myself speak in the last 15-20 minutes? How am I doing at balancing the need to make my reflections available to the group with the need to allow space for others to share their reflections? If I am over-contributing, what is the source of my need to speak? If I am under-contributing, what is the source of my reluctance?"

Third, we need to bring our thinking and feeling to dialogue. What is critical is that these are present tense concepts, as opposed to what Isaacs calls "thoughting" and "felting." Much of what we bring to our usual conversations is thoughting: ideas we developed earlier and may have used many times. You can recognize this in yourself when you are in conversation and, as the other person speaks, you find yourself noting, "I have a response to that." Thoughting allows a conversation to move very quickly, and each person may get new insights from the thoughts "downloaded" by the other, but nothing is being created in the exchange. In dialogue, the slow pace, curiosity about what the other is saying, and a commitment to wait past our thoughts to see if new thinking will emerge allows for the creation of new understandings.

Conversations with strong emotional content (for example, those that challenge our attitudes or strongly-held beliefs) often produce "felting" as well as thoughting. In this case, emotions arise in the conversation that reflect a habitual response to the topic rather than an actual response to the events of the moment. Again, the slow pace and a curiosity about what we find happening within ourselves can make it possible to move past the habitual response, to a more authentic reflection of our emotions and the truths toward which they may point us.

The excellent piece by Alvarez lays out the essential dispositions, attitudes, and behaviors for dialogue. When coupled with a contemplative heart such an engagement creates the possibility of transforming the space between and among each other to imagine new ways of responding to the issues facing us both individually and as a planetary community.

These skills are needed in ourselves as we detach from the 'false programs for happiness' which are deeply embedded in our evolutionary past and to which contemplation awakens us.[34]

These skills are needed to respond out of an integral consciousness to heal the polarities in our world, develop generative conversations, and discover new ways of moving forward together.[35]

• Communal Contemplation

When I started the Institute for Communal Contemplation and Dialogue in 2002, I sensed that the time we are living in required of us a socialization of the insights of our spirituality. We are faced with the growing complexity and diversity of worldviews that are paralyzing us as a people. For many of us, the question is how can we respond in ways that reflect the best of who we are, our authentic selves, our selves rooted in Divine Loving. My own growing understanding of self through contemplative practice and the insights of how consciousness evolves and develops over time became entangled. I felt and feel that those two dynamics when they intersect offer us a possibility to move forward in new ways to respond to the crucial issues of our time.

For me there is a synergy in opening up to my more authentic self through contemplative practice and to evolving stages of consciousness as identified in Spiral Dynamics Integral (SDi), always beckoning with more expansive, diverse, and complex understandings of self and others.[36] Having committed to contemplative practice, one can then engage with others in ways that hold the possibility of imagining new ways of moving forward. Communal contemplation can help create a 'we' space where our individual ideas, insights, and beliefs are offered for the good of the whole. As they are discussed, discerned, and developed what emerges is something new not attributed to any one person but are now owned by the group and everyone participating in it. This requires a kind of listening and responsiveness well beyond how we usually participate in meetings. It requires listening and speaking from a contemplative heart.

> *The time we are living in requires us to socialize our insights which emerge from our contemplative practice.*
>
> *Engage with others in ways that hold the possibility of imagining new ways of moving forward, of creating a 'we' space.*

Communal contemplation is a process that takes time. Here are some ways you might consider to begin this process:

*Become comfortable sitting together in contemplation. This is a powerful experience. Whenever I do a program explaining contemplation I integrate 20 minutes of contemplative sitting. The response is always the same. People feel something different being together in that silence, knowing that everyone is engaged with creating that inner spaciousness to encounter Divine Loving.

*Integrate the practice of Lectio Divina with communal contemplation. Sit together in contemplation for some time preferably 20 minutes. Then focus your reflection holding a social issue. After this, engage with one aspect of that issue or perhaps one insight from one of the reflections from this book. From the grounded place of the contemplative time, open to the issue with spacious compassion releasing any energetic thoughts that have a hold on you. Share your insights. This can lead to very deep connection and compassion within the group.[37]

*Integrate contemplative practice whenever you meet with a group. When I process a group that will be discussing issues and begin with the 20-minute contemplative sitting there is a felt sense that people are listening to each other with greater openness and compassion. I slow down the pace, periodically stopping to invite people to drop down again into that contemplative spaciousness that helps free us from our belief that my way is the one right way of thinking. This helps create the possibility that something new might emerge which will resonate with the group and move the agenda forward in new ways.

*Deepen the skills of contemplative dialogue within the group gathered who are willing to engage in communal contemplation. Ask questions of inquiry and curiosity to better understand the worldview one is coming from; create an atmosphere free of judgment and blame; ponder together alternative futures which address the needs of those gathered.

One caution — communal contemplation is not a skill set. The basic assumption is that those involved are doing their own inner work. This is never easy as the more you open yourself to the workings of Divine Love within you, the more you become aware of the shadow side of your personality and how invested you are in the self that has been shaped by your cultural context. It is allowing that side of yourself to come to full consciousness and then letting it go and giving it over to Divine Mystery that frees you to begin to engage with others more out of love than fear and opens you to imagining new ways of responding.

• Education for Public Contemplation

Today, as more and more people practice contemplation the desire for communal contemplation has increased. I feel it is a beginning response to Connie FitzGerald, OCD's call to education for public contemplation. The invitation to educate for public contemplation was offered in her essay, "The Transformation in Wisdom, the Subversive Character and Educative Power of Sophia and Contemplation." She asks:

> Is it time for a public contemplation, public education for contemplative prayer, that is, the integration into public life and education of a societal understanding of the contemplative process of transformation rather than a contemplative life largely hidden in the cloisters, hermitages and ashrams of the world, muted by those who fear...the evolutionary power of mystical transformation?[38]

Public contemplation is a profound re-education of human desire and consciousness so needed at this time in the earth's evolutionary process. It is not to be confused with praying publicly, with Christian nationalism, the blending of church and state, or a political agenda. It is at once 'the what we do and the how we do it.' There are not two actions — contemplation and action. It is one response from wholeness, from Love.

With contemplation, there are no longer walls separating the experience of God, of self, and of the world. Everything is entangled. Understanding that we live in an entangled universe doesn't make it easier for those of us who honor our faith or spiritual impulses as real. The challenge is in how we understand and reflect upon our spiritual insights and our beliefs entangled with evolution, science, the development of consciousness, and other realities of a post-modern world.

It is the capacity to hold the larger picture, so we can move together into the future.

Public contemplation is a profound re-education of human desire and consciousness so needed at this time in Earth's evolutionary process.

The challenge in Connie's words might be framed in how can we become educators for public contemplation:

> Those who teach ... need to understand and believe in the transformative character of the contemplative process inasmuch as this process is integral not only to fully developed humanity, but also to the new form of human existence struggling to be born, therefore, to the continued evolutionary thrust of the earth and the universe.
>
> [We] need to know how to educate for contemplation and transformation if the earth is to be nurtured, if the people are to be delivered from the scapegoating oppression of all kinds of violence, and if humanity is to fill its role in ushering in the next era of life on earth. This may be the most basic challenge of religion today: ... education for a transformative contemplation, which would radically affect human motivation, consciousness, desire, and, ultimately, every other area of human life and endeavor.[39]

How we respond to those insights is critical. The issues that separate us are increasing as we become more conscious of how racial, sexual, and gender bias, economic inequality, war, and the exploitation of the world's resources have influenced and shaped various structures within which we live. These abuses in our systems are becoming visible and no longer tolerated. The complexity is great. On the contemplative path we can begin to imagine new responses to the polarities we are facing. We can grow in our capacity to hold the larger picture so we can move into the future together.

And so Connie asks:

> And what would we have to do to achieve this if we believed it? What would educators in our schools and colleges do? What would business leaders meeting to discuss how to break the cycle of violence and bolster the economic vitality of our cities do? What agenda would politicians pursue? What would women's groups do? Where would Church leaders put their energies? What would each one of us do if we believed in the enormous power of contemplative transformation, transformation in Beloved Sophia?[40]

What will we do? Where will we begin? We can be leaders and schedule time at meetings to explore together through communal contemplative dialogue how we live the Gospel in this entangled universe. How are we being called to witness to Jesus' command to love our neighbor as ourselves? How would we answer who is our neighbor? How do we address the needs today of those Jesus embraced and loved — the poor, the hungry, the homeless, the sick, the despised, the imprisoned, the lonely, and the abandoned?

How do we respond from our God-selves, imagining responses that move us forward together?

Remembering Christopher Fry's words:

> *Affairs are now soul size.*
> *The enterprise is exploration into God.*
> *Where are you making for? It takes*
> *So many thousand years to wake,*
> *But will you wake for pity's sake.*

Let us begin!

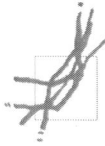

SPACIOUSNESS TO CREATE

Take time to breathe and enter the spaciousness of your heart.
Sit in contemplation, setting the intention to be open to Divine Love within you. After twenty minutes, how does it feel? Bring expression to it creatively through words, drawing, poetry, doodle, or ...

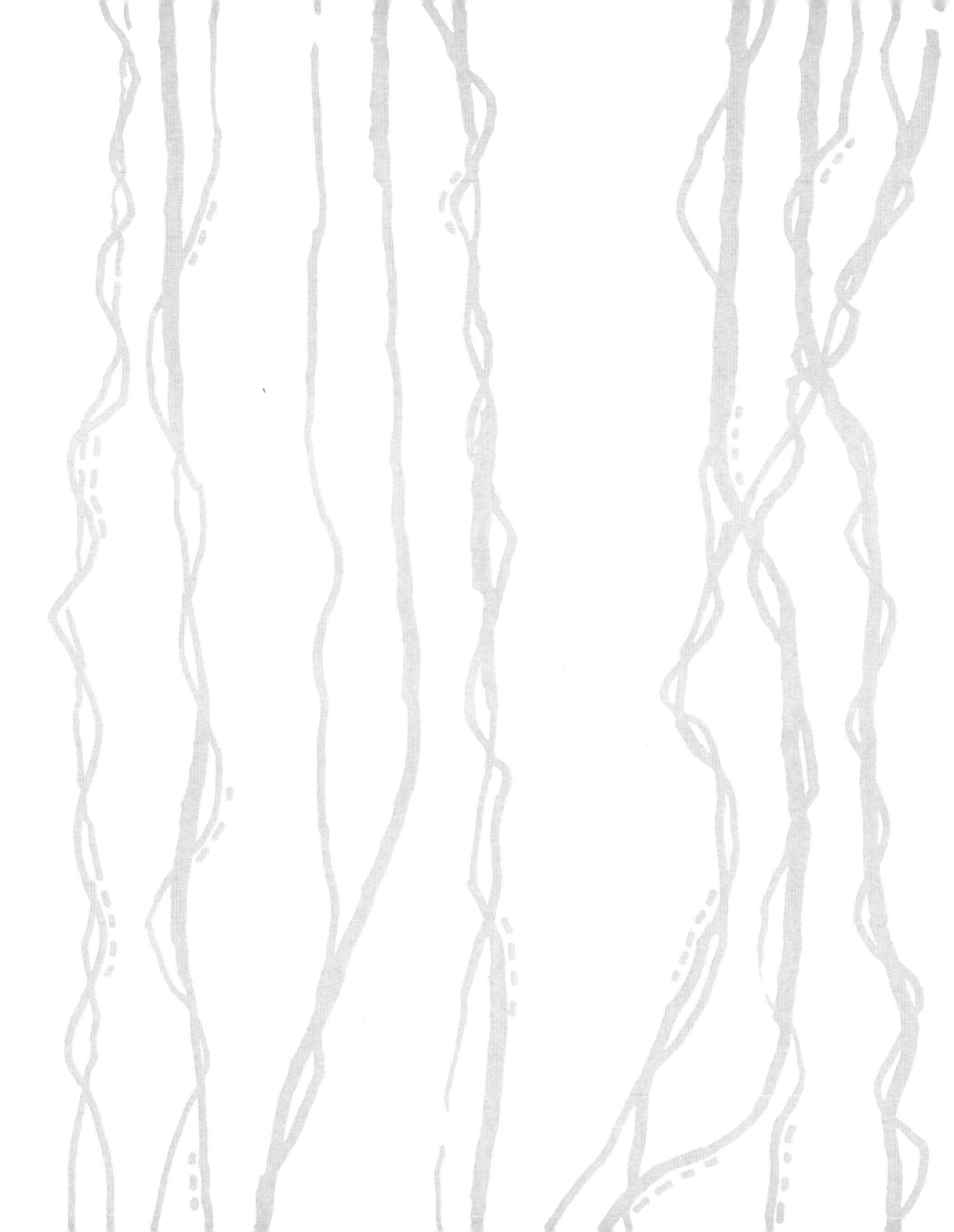

Gallery 3:

SEEING THE "REAL" OF OUR TIMES

This gallery room invites you to take a contemplative look at some of the more difficult issues facing us. These are areas of our lives that demand a new way of seeing. Many of the injustices displayed in this room have a complex history involving a dominant culture and worldviews that have excluded persons and exploited the resources of our Earth Home. These issues are calling for new responses, ones that come from a transformed consciousness.

- **A Healthy Planet is the Right to Life**

- **Embracing the Marias in Our Country**

- **We Have to be Carefully Taught to Hate**

- **Learning from the Pandemic**

- **Clerical Abuse of Children and Women**

- **Violence Permeating Our Daily Life**

• A Healthy Planet is the Right to Life

I remember seeing Greta Thunberg on a 2019 cover of Time magazine. Greta is a Swedish young woman who has spoken out and encouraged students to strike for climate change. She has spoken to the U.K. Parliament, the U.N. Climate Change COP24 conference in Poland, the World Economic Forum in Davos, Switzerland, and has met the pope. Many young people see the climate change issue as an intergenerational injustice. They don't believe that the older generations are doing enough to address it. Thunberg believes that "once we start behaving as if we were in an existential crisis, then we can avoid a climate and ecological breakdown. ... But the opportunity to do so will not last for long. We have to start today." Greta — young people — are asking us to think differently. They're asking us, the older generations, to let go of our myopic view of who we are, why we are here, what we care about, and to expand our consciousness.

Indeed, climate change is not just an individual crisis; rather, it is the collective, communal crisis for all of us living on our Earth home. Climate change seen in this way brings us face to face with the core questions of every human person:
> Who are we?
>> Why are we here?
>>> What do we care about?

Who are we? To address climate change, we cannot see ourselves isolated within our own 'tribe,' be it race, gender, nationality, or even species. This existential crisis asks us to see ourselves in a world-centric way. We are all connected. What we do affects the climate, and the climate is not separated by national boundaries. No wall can be built to keep us safe.

We are also connected to other species. United Nations Environment Programme addresses the great variety of living species — at least 8 million that we know

---

An existential crisis is a moment at which an individual questions if one's life has meaning, purpose, or value.

Climate Change brings us face to face with the core questions of every human person:
Who are we?
Why are we here?
What do we care about?

of, and there could be more — that make up our life-supporting safety net providing our food, clear water, air, energy, and more. It forecasts that one million species may be pushed to extinction in the next few years. The UN Environment Programme also speaks to how our forests, oceans, and other parts of nature soak up 60% of global fossil fuel emissions every year. A secure biosphere protects the climate and acts as a buffer to extreme weather events.

Reflecting on who we are at this time invites us to recognize our connection to other sentient and non-sentient beings, to become conscious of how nature works to enhance life on Earth and for all species. Bringing these realizations to contemplation releases our fears of the "other" and our sense of separation. It offers a new way of understanding that we are all creatures sharing in the life of God, Divine Mystery.

Why are we here? *Reflecting on why we are* here invites us to see ourselves as active participants in bringing about the *kindom* of God.[41] Bringing these realizations to contemplation opens our hearts to know God in new ways, to expand our capacity to love, and to be willing to serve the evolutionary process, bringing the fullness of life to our planet.

What do we care about? That question needs to be rethought in a culture that has prized consumerism, wealth, and individualism above all other values. Depression and suicide rates among young people continue to rise. Although there are many contributing factors, I believe the absence of having something to live for that is greater than one's self is certainly one. The health of our Earth home is a valuable, inspirational goal to which each and every one of us can contribute.

Reflecting on what we care about invites us to examine whether we make economic and political choices that value biodiversity, renewable energy, and a healthy environment — so as to move us toward a fossil-fuel-free world. Bringing these realizations to contemplation releases in us a willingness to live for something greater than ourselves, to live in ways that will ensure that future generations will live life fully.

The call of young people for climate change is the call from the future — the future generations who want to live. It has a claim on all of us — right now! It is the claim to work for the right to life for our Earth home.

> Once we start to think about the kind of world we are leaving to future generations, we look at things differently; we realize that the world is a gift which we have freely received and must share with others. ... Intergenerational solidarity is not optional, but rather a basic question of justice, since the world we have received also belongs to those who will follow us.
>
> Pope Francis[42]

• Embracing the Marias in Our Country

Not like the brazen giant of Greek fame,
With conquering limbs astride from land to land;
Here at our sea-washed, sunset gates shall stand
A mighty woman with a torch, whose flame
Is the imprisoned lightning, and her name
Mother of Exiles. From her beacon-hand
Glows world-wide welcome; her mild eyes command
The air-bridged harbor that twin cities frame.
"Keep, ancient lands, your storied pomp!" cries she
With silent lips. "Give me your tired, your poor,
Your huddled masses yearning to breathe free,
The wretched refuse of your teeming shore.
Send these, the homeless, tempest-tost to me,
I lift my lamp beside the golden door!"

> **... A mighty woman with a torch, whose flame is the imprisoned lightning, and her name Mother of Exiles.**

The words inscribed at the base of the Statue of Liberty, taken from the poem "The New Colossus" by Emma Lazarus, invites us to a compassion that is needed more than ever.

On a trip to New York City, I met a young woman. Let's call her Maria. We were waiting for the M60 bus, which would take us from LaGuardia Airport to the West Side of Manhattan in about the same time as a cab — and for much less money and less wear and tear on the planet. As we boarded the crowded bus, we ended up next to each other and began a conversation. As we talked, I was taken with her lovely smile and calm demeanor. She said she was studying to be a nurse. I felt she would be a good nurse, caring and attentive to those with whom she worked.

Maria leaves her home in the Bronx at 5 a.m. to board a train and then a bus to get to work on time an hour and a half later. She helps her mother with the day-to-day chores, and I could see she worries about her father, who in his late 50s continues to work in heavy construction.

Her mother had complications with Maria's birth in Mexico. When Maria was about 9 months old and began to try to walk, her parents realized there was something wrong with her hip. Her parents were not able to find any doctors who could address this where they lived in Mexico, so they moved to the States to get help for her. She has a limp today but is grateful to be walking. Her parents never moved on to get citizenship. She wishes they had but said she understands.

We talked DACA and the DREAM Act; she smiled and gently mused, "They won't let us all in."[43] She mentioned another bill she has heard about that would let Dreamers seek citizenship after 10 or 12 years. During that time, however, if they get even a parking ticket, they would be deported. She proudly stated that she has never gotten a ticket. Then she smiled and added, "Perhaps if I went out more with friends, I might have gotten a parking ticket."

When we parted, we hugged. I felt our meeting was a gift. I don't usually strike up a conversation when I'm traveling; yet if we hadn't, I would not have had the opportunity to hear her story. Maria is among the 800,000 Dreamers who are trying to get an education and contributing to our society while preparing to take their rightful place within the country that has been their home for most of their lives.

Many say times have changed. And that is true. Yet the words inscribed at the base of the Statue of Liberty are a continuous reminder and invitation to open ourselves to the cries of the other Marias in our nation. These words expressed our greatness as a nation in 1903, let them continue to have meaning today. Take a moment to again slowly read the poem, pondering how we might raise the lamp beside the golden door.

• We Have to be Carefully Taught to Hate

As I reflected on the violent demonstration that resulted from the white supremacist and neo-Nazis march in Charlottesville, Virginia, in 2017, the lyrics of a song in "South Pacific" by Rogers and Hammerstein came to mind. It is a song that isn't always on the list of top tunes of that musical. It is sung by a U.S. officer who is falling in love with a young native woman and is struggling with his feelings toward her. The words that have always haunted me are: 'You've got to be taught to hate ... you've got to be carefully taught before it's too late ... before you are 7 or 8...'

I found myself saying over and over, you've got to be carefully taught, as I watched the coverage of Charlottesville and the violence began. I was sickened as I saw the bottles being thrown at those who came to stand in nonviolent opposition to the white nationalists, the Klan, and the alt-right. It is hard for me to understand how there are still people who believe that the United States of America is and should be a white nation. Or perhaps, I don't want to believe this about fellow citizens.

It is a worldview well-expressed in that 1949 musical. You've got to be taught to hate and fear. That teaching happens consciously and unconsciously. I began to reflect: when do we begin to see color as a defining characteristic indicating inferiority or superiority? When do we look at noses, lips, hair, and body shapes and formulate judgments about what kind of person s/he is? When do we hear grammar and voice intonations as signs of one's level of education or upbringing? When do we no longer see individuals but only perceive them as a group that is threatening a way of life? When do we learn to be afraid and hate the other?

Who teaches us that? So many people and in so many ways. As the song says, you have to be taught before it is too late ... before 7 or 8.

— *How can we be untaught?*

The question for us is: How can we be untaught? Perhaps it need not be said that such un-teaching would involve how the media portrays difference, what is taught in schools, and how churches speak about race and religion. But it has to touch more deeply into our very being.

We need to see with new eyes and hear with new ears. We need 'to take a long, loving look at the real.' We have work to be done if we are to survive and thrive as a loving, relational community of great and complex diversity. What obstacles are you aware of in yourself to seeing that we are all one?

This is hard work. Contemplative practice helps us do this. It helps us get in touch with how we are all one and more similar than different. It helps us become aware of our biases so rooted in culture and familial beliefs. It helps us surrender to the Divine working within us to teach us who we really are in this planetary community. What is arising in you as you reflect on what needs to be untaught?

• Learning from the Pandemic

Where were you when the coronavirus hit?[44] A question we often ask ourselves as we recall a major incident that has occurred in our life. Perhaps when we recall the coronavirus the better question will be: What did you learn from the coronavirus pandemic?

Each of us experienced the pandemic differently, and yet we all experienced it. Whether one of our loved ones died or became very sick, or whether we were spared that grief, we could not escape the suffering of so many. The count became staggering as both the death toll and the number of those infected mounted. And it wasn't just in one city. It was throughout our country, and it wasn't just our country, it was throughout the world.

We couldn't escape the reports of those whose jobs were lost and for whom being at home brought added worry about paying bills and securing food and shelter. Still others were alone with an abusive partner, exacerbated by the lockdown. And still, others were locked inside themselves — alone, desperate, and depressed, perhaps relying on drugs to keep them company.

Like a blanket the virus wrapped around the Earth community and forced us to focus on these difficult realities; and as we did, we saw gaping wounds beneath the spread of the virus. Although we were all potential victims, some of us were more so. The inequities of our health care system and our economic system were exposed through the disproportionate spread of the disease among people of color. The inequities of our international economic arrangements led to a disproportionate burden on many less-wealthy countries, which were unable to obtain vaccinations for their people. The economic toll of the lockdowns throughout the world exacerbated food shortages, increasing the number of children suffering from malnutrition. At so many levels, the

As often happens when one begins to treat a wound, other underlying conditions are brought to the surface.

tentacles of the virus extended and intertwined with various structures and systems — revealing much greater sickness than simply Covid-19.

As often happens when one begins to treat a wound, other underlying conditions are brought to the surface. The experience of police brutality, long suffered by our Black sisters and brothers, could no longer be contained. George Floyd[45] became the icon that galvanized not only people of the United States but those in other countries to take to the streets to proclaim that *Black Lives Matter*. Systemic racism demanded to be addressed.

Reflecting on all of this I found myself drawn to the Psalms. The Psalms capture so many emotions; offer poetic ways to interpret what we are experiencing; and help us see the Divine Presence in it all. I became aware that it was remembering where I was when the coronavirus hit that revealed what I learned and led me to Psalm 18.

> *You delivered me from prejudice and intolerance;*
> *You opened my heart to all nations;*
> *People whom I had not known befriended me.*[46]

The coronavirus became "real" to me in early March of 2020 toward the end of a pilgrimage I was on with Future Church.[47] Our group had gone from being strangers to a real community. We were careful and sanitized our hands all the time. We felt safe and tried to keep things in perspective. As we traveled from Thessaloniki to Athens, we were often the only ones at the hotels we stayed in, at the restaurants, and at the various archeological sites.

When we arrived at the hotel in Athens and went to dinner, things changed. When I entered a very full restaurant, I was caught off guard. All of a sudden looking at these "others" from various countries, I realized the implications of what had now been called a pandemic. For a moment I felt all these "others" were the potential carriers of the virus. Certainly not our group of twenty-nine.

I became aware of how very quickly a group can become a tribe and the "others" become those from whom you need to protect yourself and your group. The "others" might even become the cause of whatever is happening and thus become the scapegoat.

However, as I began to reflect on the reality of the virus and trying to contain it, it became clear that no matter what my group and I might be doing to stay healthy, it wasn't enough. I had to trust that everyone else in the restaurant was also committed to washing their hands and the other preventive measures we were asked to practice. If any of us were to have the virus, we would all be quarantined.

I could feel the web that was woven around everyone in the dining room. We were all interconnected and on this journey together. The feeling was quite visceral.

It is too easy to fall into unconscious patterns of blaming the "other" — the "Kung Flu" virus, the "Chinese" virus — it is their fault. Contemplation invites you into a spaciousness to stay awake and alert to reactions that are intolerant or prejudicial. It invites you to be open to the unexpected stranger who offers you compassion.

> *For I pursued my fears and faced them;*
> *And did not run back until I was free.*
> *I saw each one through, so that they were not able to rise;*
> *They were transformed by love.*[48]

Fears abound with such uncertainty. How long will it last? Will I be able to pay my bills? What if I get sick? How long will I be separated from the people I love, especially the elders? Will there be enough food and other essentials? Will I have a job? Will I have my business? What about my future income or my savings? What will the future be for my children and grandchildren?

Other emotions — resentment, anger, deep sadness, frustration — rose as we faced events that normally enrich our lives being disrupted: weddings that were upended after months of planning; college and high school diplomas awarded through the mail; trips saved for over the years canceled; birthdays, anniversaries, sporting events, concerts, plays, conferences and meetings that never happened.

The Psalmist says for us to pursue our fears and face them. Great advice since we know that negative emotions cause stress and illness if they are not acknowledged. As counterintuitive as it seems, to face those emotions and fears, and embrace them, helps release their power over you and their negative effect on you.

It is useless to try to stop feeling such emotions or to feel you shouldn't have them for many reasons. Repressing or rejecting them often keeps them simmering just below the surface. Contemplative practices invite us to intentionally lean into the feeling, even intensify it, and transform it with a loving heart. The Welcoming Prayer, which is part of Centering Prayer is a practice worth trying to see if it might help at this time.[49]

> *Yet there was no safe haven, no hiding place from fear.*
> *Then the channels of the sea were seen,*
> *And the foundations of the world laid bare,*
> *The earth gave a mighty shudder*
> *Then settled down to heal in the Silence.*[50]

It seems as if our earth is giving a mighty shudder. We know that our economic and political systems have become dysfunctional. As a people, too many of us in industrialized countries consume more than is necessary. Individualism has dwarfed concern for the common good. The climate crisis continues to intensify. The old ways do not work anymore.

We need a new consciousness to imagine new ways of responding to the many crises we are experiencing.

As the Earth settles down to heal in "the Silence," perhaps we can come together across the ideological divide to sit together in silence. In that space, we would begin to share our deepest longings and hopes for how to be an Earth community for this millennium. Having stopped doing so much of what we take for granted, we may be willing to emerge from our healing in new ways — creating structures to provide a more equitable distribution of revenue and resources for all.

> *I abandon myself to You, O Living Presence, My strength.*
> *You are my rock, my stronghold, My freedom...*
> *I call upon You, Heart of my heart,*
> *Singing praises to your Name,*
> *And fear no longer holds me.*[51]

Contemplation is setting the intention to be open to the workings of the Divine within oneself. Let us pray that we learn through our experience of the pandemic the stark realization that we are all connected; that when we face into our fears, we can transform them through love; and that we emerge from it all committed to a new way of being and acting. What fears arise in you that you need to transform through love?

• Clerical Abuse of Children and Women

It is difficult to find the words to capture what I feel as reports of sexual abuse by Catholic priests are revealed. The number of priests and the number of children and others abused is staggering. In the victims' testimonies, one feels the pain and the shame even many years later. The magnitude of the violation is hard to imagine when the victim sees the abuser as a representative of God.

I felt I wanted to bring the victims to prayer and chose the contemplative practice of Tonglen so beautifully taught by Pema Chodron.[52] Engaging in this practice, I tried to breathe in the feeling of their pain. I experienced the heaviness of a boulder pressed against my chest; darkness all around; tightness of my body; cornered with no escape. Then I imagined gifts I sensed they needed. I breathed out the image of a mother cradling her infant child with unconditional love; a field full of wildflowers creating a safe space for them to play; and a gentle healing embrace of Divine Mystery. Breathe in the pain. Breathe out the gifts.

As I reflected on all this, something else kept trying to emerge within me and wouldn't leave me. At first it was anger over the abuse of power in the church. Power when exercised through the lens of a hierarchical system classifies people according to relative importance. Those deemed more important often dominate those considered lesser, requiring them to do things they would not choose to do.

Those dominated know they will be punished or suffer serious consequences if they don't comply. For too many centuries, the complement to such a worldview has been the belief that men hold the power and women are largely excluded from it and are to be submissive to men. Both of these views are operative in the Catholic Church.

> *Bring the victims to prayer ...*
> *the contemplative practice of Tonglen*
>
> *Power is abused when exercised through the lens of a hierarchical system that classifies people according to relative importance.*

Then my anger deepened as I thought about how these assumptions about the inferiority of women have been dangerously coupled within the official church in terms of its teaching about sexuality.

The primary purpose of sexual intercourse always understood within marriage was to ensure the continuation of the species and male lineage. The woman was to submit to her husband's sexual demands without question. This integration of conscious and unconscious assumptions, values, beliefs and behaviors created an untenable position for many Catholics, and especially for women.

Given the insights of contemporary psychology, theology, science and spirituality, many women refuse to be seen as inferior to men or submissive to male power. They understand the beauty of one's sexuality and know they are equally as capable as men to make decisions and act as moral agents, especially when it comes to decisions relating to their sexuality.

At first, these thoughts seemed so tangled, and yet as I read once again about the abuse of children by priests, I know it is all related. Unhealthy understanding of one's body, one's sexuality; power over and male superiority; and the belief that women are less than men are interlocked world views.

And so I asked myself how can I embrace all of this in a contemplative way. Surprisingly, the whole hierarchy of pope, cardinal, bishop, monsignor, priest, and deacon … appeared in my mind. I felt it was a challenge but also an invitation.

I recognized that although certain policies and procedures have been put in place to prevent such horrific abuse from happening again, that doesn't necessarily transform the worldview or the consciousness that permits and allows such behavior. That only comes with grace and prayer.

I decided to bring the whole hierarchical male clergy as a collective to my Tonglen practice.

At first, it was difficult to see them as victims. But then I saw them as victims of a different order. Clericalism within the patriarchal, hierarchical structure perpetuates the misuse of power, and clerics' complicity in that mindset makes them both a victim and a perpetrator of abusive behavior. I pictured the male clerics and tried to breathe in the pain that such a worldview inflicts on its perpetrators. I felt the tight constriction of my throat; the weight of centuries pressing down; stomach cramps fighting inner fears; and darkness enveloping me.

I then tried to imagine what gifts were needed. I breathed out the images of chains falling away that have bound them to this worldview; Pentecost fire opening minds and hearts to see in new ways; a humility that invites a profound prostration asking forgiveness and signaling transformation; and a courage to let go of all the privileged trappings. Breathe in the pain. Breathe out the gifts.

I sense I will do this practice more than once. I believe that by doing this practice and sending gifts of transformation to the clerical members of our church, something will be transformed in them and in me as well. Fundamentally, I believe the clerical church is in search of its soul.

I also recall something that is always said: The church is human. Perhaps this scandal will help us to claim our humanity as the church, the people of God, inviting us all to reimagine how to live into our future.

• Violence Permeating Our Daily Life

A friend and I often go to lunch at a nearby fast-food restaurant. The other day two little girls we had seen before were sitting in a booth. Their mother works at the restaurant and brought her daughters to work with her.

This time the oldest girl, about 5, was holding roses and a 'Happy Birthday' helium balloon. We asked if it was her birthday. Without hesitation, she said no, it was the birthday of her sister, who had been shot and killed. She planned to release the balloon into the sky so her sister in heaven could enjoy it. She then said that her father had been killed as well and was in heaven taking care of her older sister.

How can it be that violence so permeates our society that little children matter-of-factly say that someone they love has been shot and killed? Recall Sandy Hook[53] where twenty children between 6 and 7 years old were murdered in 2012. Many of us thought that would be the mass shooting that would turn our nation away from violence. This horrendous act would create the necessary groundswell to enact good gun legislation and address mental health in this country. Sadly, that has not been the case. Mass shootings in the United States have nearly tripled since 2013, the year after Sandy Hook.

We encountered this little girl the same week that we heard about five Memphis police officers who savagely beat to death Tyre Nichols, a young Black man they pulled over for a traffic violation. Nichols was beaten to death by the very men we expect to protect us.

We live in a culture of violence — despite millennia of experience that confirms violence does not bring lasting peace.

We can act to change this culture of violence. We can support policies and legislation that address access to

---

How can it be that violence so permeates our society that little children matter-of-factly say that someone they love has been shot and killed?

We live in a culture of violence — despite millennia of experience that confirms violence does not bring lasting peace.

guns and address mental health concerns to name just a couple of needed responses.

We must attend to another dimension as well. The violence that surrounds us and the suffering it causes erode our inner life. Hopeless, angry, powerless, we can't make sense of it all. We wonder where Divine Mystery is in all this. We feel alone in this violent world of our making. We acknowledge our complicity and don't know what to do.

Perhaps our ancestors in faith can offer us some help. What did they do when they couldn't make sense of things? They lamented.

The Hebrew Scriptures' Book of Lamentations is a poetic book that mourns the destruction of Jerusalem and the suffering of the Jewish people at the hands of the Babylonians. As a prayer form, a lamentation is a passionate expression of grief, sorrow and repentance.

Recall how Jesus lamented the day he died, saying, "Eli, Eli, lema sabachthani?" — "My God, my God, why have you forsaken me?" (Matthew 27:46). Even in the midst of acknowledging that pain, Jesus surrendered in love and gave up his spirit. Jesus trusted Love in the midst of it all, even when it looked hopeless.

When we lament, we cry out: weep, howl, and mourn. We speak our sufferings aloud to God, however we experience Divine Mystery. In this way, we can get in touch with the suffering of the world and cry out — weeping, howling, and mourning for all.

We can write lamentations using language and words that embody what we feel. Pray it aloud. Let it be loud in you. Get exhausted with your weeping. Grieve the reality.

When finished, take the time to sit. Feel your tiredness and emptiness. Begin to breathe deeply; allow the air to enter and move down deeply into your belly. Continue breathing, allowing more air to enter and expand within you. Set the intention to be present to God, Divine Loving, and continue to breathe for 5 to 10 minutes. Allow space to open within you. Simply be present, sensing and trusting, as Jesus did, love in the midst of it all.

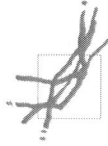

SPACIOUSNESS TO CREATE

Take time to breathe and enter the spaciousness of your heart.

For a period of time, sit in contemplation, setting the intention to be open to Divine Love within you. With your contemplative gaze, reflect on your experience in Gallery Three. Was anything evoked in you, became present to you, challenged, or shifted in you? Bring expression to it creatively through words, drawing, poetry, doodle, or ...

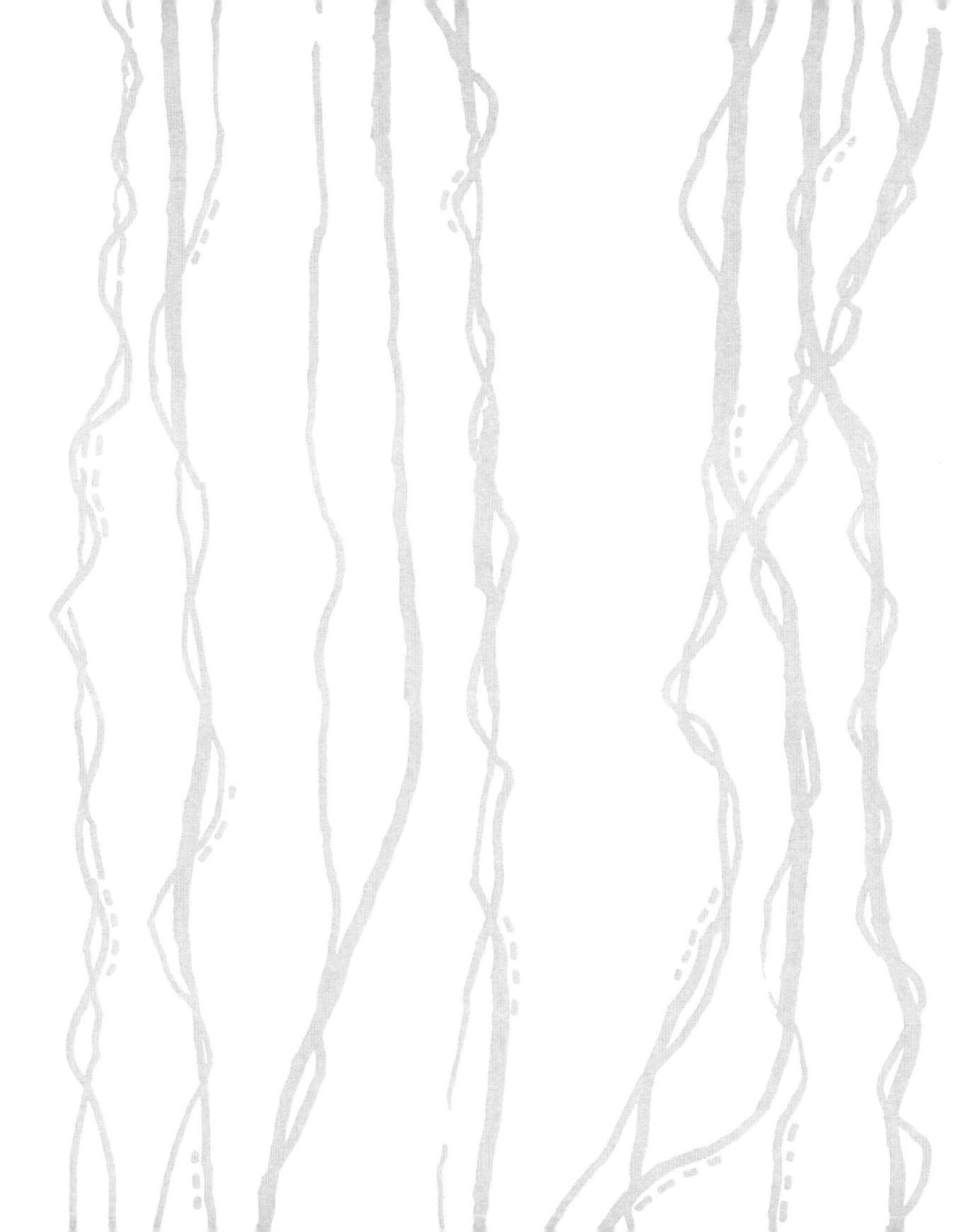

Gallery 4:

PUBLIC LIFE AND DEMOCRACY

As you move into this next area of the art gallery the reflections take a broader look at the issues which are affecting us. The increasing polarities we are experiencing especially within our country are calling for us to take a long loving look at what is happening. We are faced with needing transformational leaders; people committed to healing the polarization among us; a reinventing of our democratic principles, values, and structures; and an understanding of how our faith calls us to action on behalf of social justice.

- **With Great Diversity, We Are Still One Nation**

- **Walking a Tightrope to Reinvent Our Democracy**

- **This Moment Needs Transformational Leaders**

- **When the Future is Obscure, You Need Radical Trust**

- **Go Back and Fetch It**

- **Can Christians Be Progressive? Absolutely!**

• With Great Diversity, We Are Still One Nation

I have always loved maps. I remember how in grade school we had to draw the outline of each state for geography class and learn what that state produced that contributed to the overall economy. I loved opening up a neatly folded map to navigate a road trip with a yellow marker showing the way. There was something comforting and amazing knowing that someone had traversed the country finding all these roads, rivers, cities, towns, and landmarks. Looking at the entire map gave me a sense of how all these individual states with their shapes and geological identities were part of a whole. Bordered by the Pacific and Atlantic oceans, Canada, and Mexico, we were the United States of America.

Because my work involves quite a bit of travel, I often find myself on airplanes. Sitting by the window allows me to see the various terrains of the country. When I have the opportunity to fly across the country on a clear day, I watch the cities give way to farmland to open fields to cattle country to mountains to the coast with small towns sprinkled throughout.

I never tire of it. It provides a perspective drawing me beyond my boundaries of place. I realize that there is such diversity, but all within one country.

These memories came back to me as I flew across the country recently. It was a clear day and a morning flight. However, when I stood for a stretch break, I was dismayed by what I saw. Throughout the whole plane, daylight was not to be seen. All the window shades were closed. Everyone was watching their personal video screen with their individual choice of a show.

We were all separate and distinct ... we could be anywhere ... going anywhere.

What came to mind was the work of historian Colin Woodard, who posits that North America is made up of

> *Flying across the country ... realizing that there was such diversity, but it was all within one country.*
>
> *We need to reimagine how our differences could strengthen our pluralistic democracy and address anew both individual liberty and the common good.*

eleven distinct nations, each with its unique historical roots and cultures developed over the years.[54] Woodard also explores how the struggle between individual liberty and the common good contributed to these divisions and has been the basis of nearly every major disagreement in our history.

This analysis is an interesting backdrop to our current naming of states along political persuasions: red, blue, or purple. The struggle between two basic values of the United States — individual liberty and the common good — continues.

It not only continues, but has intensified as we, as a nation, have become more diverse in race, religion, language, gender, country of origin, educational achievement, and economic status. Individual liberty and the common good are increasingly at odds with each other.

Our differences have become more distinct and the question that is stirring underneath is whether we are still one country.

Rethinking what we assume about our differences as a nation and what behaviors keep us from engaging in dialogue with those who think differently is critical to our future. An awareness and freedom to respond in new ways flow from a contemplative heart.

Our contemplative practice awakens us to see our connection to the land we inhabit, and to be in awe of its diversity as well as the diversity among all of us who live on the land. We create spaciousness to reimagine how our differences could strengthen our pluralistic democracy, and how moving toward understanding might shift what possibilities could emerge for addressing anew both individual liberty and the common good.

I'm not sure what it will take for us to begin but perhaps we can start by opening up the shades when we are on a plane and take a look out the window to see where we are and where we are going. We might take the time to sense how we are part of the land and each other. We could look at the people around us and not just the video screen or the screen on our phones. We might ponder the what-ifs and help make them a reality.

Let us deepen our contemplative practice to embrace our underlying unity as a people and as a nation and behave in the ways necessary to forge a future that is respectful of both individual rights and the common good. 'Taking a long loving look,' what do you see as you look across our nation? What can you imagine…

• Walking a Tightrope to Reinvent Our Democracy

Over the past years, we've witnessed a dismantling of the scaffolding that has held in place the structures, values, assumptions, precedents, and norms of our democratic institutions. The bonds of trust among us about the democratic process have been severely frayed and, in some cases, broken.

After the results of the 2020 election were finalized, the divisions, the disruption, and the torn pieces of our democracy were still there. Opposing sides solidified and democracy itself became the victim as we witnessed an unprecedented, organized attack on the U.S. Capitol and our democratic values, on Jan. 6, 2021.

The image I have is that between these deepening divisions is stretched the tightrope of democracy, and the future depends on those of us who are willing to walk it to reinvent our democracy. Reinvent is defined as producing something new that is based on something that already exists.

Reinvention is a formidable challenge. Our Constitution signed in 1787, with our Bill of Rights ratified in 1791, has shaped our democratic structures and our identity as citizens. Today we are growing in our realization that the interpretation of the original values was shaped primarily by those who were in power and who belonged to the dominant race, class, gender, and religion. It is becoming clearer to many that the laws and policies and the interpretation of our history have been distorted. There is a desire and an outcry to change that — to lance the wound of systemic injustice that has been hurting our country.

How these documents are interpreted reveals the tensions and differences among us as a nation throughout the years. They spark partisan debates and protest

> *Those of us committed to reinvent our democracy will be walking a tightrope.*
>
> *With the breakdown of trust in our democratic processes, it is not clear to me whether there will be enough confidence and willingness to risk that a pluralistic democracy can bring us together.*

movements on both the left and the right. But through it all, respect for each other and belief that all are working toward the common good got us through some very tense times of great division.

Today, the question is whether that can happen again. With the breakdown of trust in our democratic processes, it is not clear to me whether there will be enough confidence and willingness to risk that a pluralistic democracy can bring us together.

Those of us committed to reinvent our democracy will be walking a tightrope. We need to reinvent our democracy and yet we face the possibility of falling on either side of the tightrope. We will need to be agile and awake. We will need to be aware of who we are and how we have been shaped over these many years — for good and for ill.

Key to reinvention is to restore the trust that has been eroded. We need to recommit to the underlying ethical principles of our democratic system: truthfulness, justice/fairness and temperance/respect for rights of others.[55] Key is to honor and protect the self-governing principles that are the foundation of our democracy's rule of law.

This is made more difficult when sides are taken and both sides or multiple sides claim a moral imperative.

The work that I have been doing in integral theory and spiral dynamics challenges me to understand the different stages of consciousness from which people respond to these critical concerns.[56] I need to be in touch with what I believe and why and where I sense within me an opening for change. Curiosity and open-ended questions help me to envision new ways of responding. We need to communicate with each other if a new possibility is to emerge.

Part of moving forward is to recognize both the humanity of those who have been privileged and whose behavior and values have been normative and to advocate for the inclusion of those excluded: their rights, values, beliefs, and perspectives. Such an alchemy might bring about transformation.

Remembering that we are all made in the image and likeness of God, Divine Mystery, and that our human nature is fundamentally good helps us keep our balance. For those beliefs help us truly respect the other even as difficult things are said that need to be heard.

Perhaps most needed to keep our balance is an alignment with a strong magnetic center. In contemplative prayer, we are drawn toward the magnetic center where Divine Mystery dwells. We come to this place within us where we are aligned with Divine Love. Such an alignment will keep us balanced as we walk into the future open to new possibilities for the future of our democracy. Bring yourself into the presence of Divine Mystery. See what emerges as to where you are on the tightrope.

• This Moment Needs Transformational Leaders

A transactional leadership style is evident in multiple areas of our lives these days. Watching it play out among so many within our government continues to greatly disturb me. Making choices only when the outcome will benefit the person, or his or her political party, seems to reflect one of the earliest stages of Maslow's hierarchy of needs — commonly described as "you scratch my back, I'll scratch yours."

This style of transactional leadership is also described as that which does not look to change the future; rather it keeps things the same. It best motivates people for the short term with a system of rewards and punishments, paying attention to their followers' work to find faults and deviations from the norm.

This type of leadership certainly has existed through the centuries. However, today, the global community is faced with challenges that demand imaginative and selfless leaders who can address the breakdown of the economic, political, cultural, and religious structures/systems that have served us in the past.

In many situations, the very values and beliefs embodied in these systems which have been so helpful in the past are now lived out in extreme ways. For example, take market capitalism which has brought many societies out of poverty, and developed in many of us a pride in our individuality and achievements. It is now contributing to the unequal distribution of wealth among and within nations and has raised up individualism to the sacrifice of any consideration of the common good. Our future needs transformational leaders. Leaders who won't sacrifice our future for what is best for them. Leaders who acknowledge that we can't go back but call us forth to a new sense of altruism and the common good.

Science and mysticism might offer us some help in

> *Leaders who acknowledge that we can't go back but call us forth to a new sense of altruism and the common good.*
>
> *Today, the global community is faced with challenges that demand imaginative and selfless leaders who can address the breakdown of the various structures/systems that have served us in the past.*

this area.[57] The classical scientific worldview in which we have been immersed over the past centuries with its linear, mechanistic, and atomistic paradigm of Newtonian physics, has shaped and influenced our thinking in all areas of our life-economics, politics, education, health care, and the like. The way we conceive of reality emphasizes separation, discrete pieces, either/or thinking, isolation, and fragmentation.

Quantum physics, which has been seeping into our lives with or without our noticing since the turn of the 20th century, complements Newtonian physics and in some cases has turned that scientific worldview upside down. Quantum physics is showing us that we are not isolated individuals, corporations, or nations going about our business like silos with no impact on anyone or anything else. Rather, we are an interconnected web of life. We are all connected and what we do affects the whole. Other breakthroughs are such that many physicists say that what quantum physics is revealing to us requires a completely new way of thinking about everything. It involves an imaginative leap.[58]

I find hope in the emergence of such a new structure of consciousness that could integrate us with the greater whole. This new consciousness, often called integral consciousness, has been described as one in which there is a capacity for paradox and ambiguity and the ability to see the whole before the parts. Such a way of seeing I believe will help us see how connected we are and how my own fulfillment depends on and contributes to the common good.

Developments in science are emerging with an old but perhaps unexpected partner in this call to a new consciousness. It is found in the mystical traditions of all the world religions. Many of those who practice contemplation and experience Divine Mystery in a more direct and intuitive way often express the insight that we are all one — we are all connected. We just are not awake to it.

Thomas Merton, a Trappist monk, famously wrote about his experience at the corner of Fourth and Walnut in Louisville, Kentucky:

> *I was suddenly overwhelmed with the realization that I loved all those people, that they were mine and I theirs, that we could not be alien to one another even though we were total strangers. It was like waking from a dream of separateness, of spurious self-isolation in a special world. ... And if only everybody could realize this! But it cannot be explained. There is no way of telling people that they are all walking around shining like the sun. ... If only they could all see themselves as they really are. If only we could see each other that way all the time. There would be no more war, no more hatred, no more cruelty, no more greed.*[59]

Constance FitzGerald, OCD, in her reflection "From Impasse to Prophetic Hope: Crisis of Memory," reflects on the importance of this kind of shift of consciousness.[60] "It is my strong suspicion that the prayer of no experience, effecting an essential change in selfhood, may be emerging with such frequency as a response to a world driven by selfishness and self-concern. Any hope for new consciousness and a self-forfeiture driven by love stands opposed by a harsh reality." After naming areas in which we act to serve our own interests — hoarding resources, ravaging the earth, scapegoating each other, killing, maiming, and torturing — she notes, "Our ability to embody our communion with every human person on the earth and our unassailable connectedness with everything living is limited." Connie then continues (we need) "to make the transition from radical individualism to a genuine synergistic community ... The future of the entire earth community is riding on whether we can find a way beyond the limits of our present evolutionary trajectory."

Such a future needs transformational leaders to call forth in us new ways of addressing the common good amid difficult choices. And such a future needs all of us to bring to our contemplative prayer the openness to move from radical individualism to genuine synergistic community.

Let us pray with Nan Merrill's interpretation of Psalm 140, which offers us a piece of contemplative wisdom.[61]

> *Are we not called to make Love conscious in our lives?*
> *To divinize the earth with heavenly splendor? ...*
> *That I might flow in harmony with the universe,*
> *and be a bearer of integrity.*
> *I know that You stand beside those who suffer,*
> *and You are the Light of those imprisoned in darkness.*
> *Surely You will guide us into the new dawn,*
> *that we may live as co-creators with You.*

• When the Future is Obscure, You Need Radical Trust

Sitting by a lake before dawn, I saw the mist obscuring the horizon. The lake was like glass. Its stillness profound. There were no sounds of the birds, squirrels, or other awakening creatures. The houses were dark and in shadow.

I felt that this morning captured for me where we are as women in religious life, as citizens in a polarized nation, and as people of faith. The future we face is shrouded in mist.

Apostolic religious life as we have known it faces an unknown future. We are like many of our foundresses and founders, who responded to the needs of their time without knowing the future of the work. Unlike them, we are living in a time when the theology and spirituality of a more traditional time has been transformed with the advent of science and the values of the modern period. The raison d'être of our lives is being transformed. We try to look beyond the aging of our communities, the lack of new members, and the closing of sponsored ministries, yet the mist is clinging to the horizon.

We face a polarized electorate in our country. There is much talk about us moving away from democracy to more autocratic leaders. Similar shifts are happening in other democratic countries. There are many reasons for this. Two that stand out for me are the failure of globalism and the racism and sexism that are embedded in many of our policies and structures of the modern era.

Globalism has failed to bring a level of economic security to everyone. In the U.S. and most of the post-industrial world, wealth is disproportionately held by a small minority. This is becoming more known and no longer tolerable.

Second, there is a growing awareness of how many of

> *The question on the horizon is whether democracy can achieve a new approach to transform a future that addresses the well-being of all of life, including our Earth home.*
>
> *In the hands of Christian nationalists religion has become an instrument of division and violence urging punitive measures to restore more traditional structures of family and economic life.*

the structures and policies put into place — to achieve the progress that has generated such wealth — systematically violated the rights and well-being of those who were not white, straight, male, Christian, or Western European.

The question on the horizon is whether democracy can achieve a new approach to transform a future that addresses the well-being of all of life, including our Earth home. As I try to see that possibility, the mist continues to hold steady, limiting my vision.

Perhaps most painful is that as people of faith, religion has become an instrument of division and violence. The growth of Christian nationalism is frightening. Much is being written about it. Herbert Kitschelt, a political scientist at Duke University, was quoted in a *New York Times* opinion article as saying that there is no social organization in America as segregated as churches.[62] His analysis described what is happening as the spread of a form of clerofascism. It advocates for "a white evangelical oligarchy with repression — jail time, physical violence, and death — inflicted on those who will not succumb to this oligarchy" and likens it to what prevailed in the South until the 1960s.

Although it seems extreme, one begins to see this approach emerging in the aftermath of the Supreme Court decision on *Roe v. Wade*. State legislatures are racing to enact punitive measures against women who are faced with challenging pregnancies. However, this is much larger than one ruling or one policy.

Kitschelt argues that those who espouse these beliefs are fighting hard to return to more traditional structures of family and economic life. This is happening globally as "right-wing populists around the world draw on religion as their ultimate ideological defense, even if their religious doctrines are seemingly different," citing Donald Trump, Vladimir Putin, Narendra Modi, Recep Tayyip Erdogan, and Xi Jinping.

For those of us who believe the religious impulse is one of love, mercy, compassion, inclusivity, and justice — and who also acknowledge that many of the values of the modern world and insights of science complement, transform, and deepen our faith — it is difficult to see where we are going as the mist remains at the horizon.

As I sat waiting for dawn, the mist began to lift. Birds flew overhead flapping their wings. Squirrels began to chatter and frolic. Slowly, the sun began to rise and soon the mist rose and the houses around the lake were illuminated.

This reminded me of a quote I received from Benedictine Br. David Steindl-Rast who led the retreat before my profession class took first vows.[63] The quote was "All we can do to make muddy water clear is to let it settle in silence."

To be still and let things settle. To be still and allow the mist to dissipate.

I don't believe that means to be passive. I believe it means to trust. Trust that actively abandons one's false self to the Divine Mystery working within. It is a trust that empowers. A trust that believes that if I sit in contemplation, the spaciousness created invites me to listen to the depths of my being. As I enter into Christ consciousness, I will know what to do, what to say, and how to say it.

The future will not be veiled in mist but rather, knowing that what each of us does is part of evolving that future, we will become like the sun, the light that burns off the mist and illuminates a future more in keeping with the kindom of God.

The call is to deepen one's contemplative practice. It is to trust in the words of Constance FitzGerald, OCD, "Contemplation is not a validation of things as they are ... but a constant questioning ... [that] believes in the coming of a transformed vision of God ... a new and integrating spirituality capable of creating a new politics and generating new social structures."[64]

• Go Back and Fetch It

"Sankofa" is a Ghanaian word that translated means "Go back and fetch it." It also refers to a mythical bird whose feet are firmly planted forward while its head is turned backward carrying a precious egg in its mouth.

It symbolizes the belief that the past serves as a guide for planning the future. It represents a people's quest for knowledge with the implication that the quest is based on critical examination and intelligent and patient investigation.

The Ghanaian people believe that there must be movement and new learning as time passes. As this forward march proceeds, the knowledge of the past must never be forgotten.

We need to ask ourselves: Do we have the will and courage to turn our head backward?

The pandemic forced us to stop. We became aware of what we take for granted in our lives. We woke up to how differently we experienced the pandemic depending on our location, economic status, health, gender, and race. These disparities revealed causes that go beyond individual negligence or group stereotypes. They revealed political policies, legal decisions, economic choices, and religious beliefs that protected and entitled a specific group in our country.

For those in power, this privileged place often obscured the injustice and damage being done by such decisions. The pandemic laid bare what has become normative over these last centuries. This past cannot be ignored or covered back over.

Can we learn from our past? Can we undertake a "quest for knowledge with the implication that the quest is based on critical examination, and intelligent and patient investigation" as the Ghanaian people believe?

Sankofa refers to a mythical bird whose feet are firmly planted forward while its head is turned backward carrying a precious egg in its mouth.

What are those "precious eggs" that we will need if we are to learn from our past and move forward together?

If yes, then what may be the "precious eggs" of our past that may have been forgotten?

As I turned my head backward I found a few of our "precious eggs."

I saw the first three words of the preamble to the Constitution: *"We the People."* Although we know that when it was first implemented it did not include everyone living in what was becoming the United States, I wondered if there is a "precious egg" there for us today.

Can these words be lived into the future where all people — regardless of race, economic status, gender identity, physical and mental ability — have access to decision making and creation of norms for a truly pluralistic United States of America?

I saw our Black sisters and brothers who experienced slavery and its generational effects holding a "precious egg" for the future. It is *one of suffering, courage and hope.* In spite of decades of having their lives stolen and their bodies broken, they continue their journey to freedom believing that this is not what should be. They have the courage to follow hope calling them forward.

Can *we the people* find strength in such wisdom as we come to terms with what should never have been, as we together honestly access how the benefits accrued so unfairly over the years can be restored in some way as we move into the future?

I saw our ancestors, our Native American brothers and sisters holding another "precious egg." They understood that *all of life is connected*. They knew that humans survive only when the rest of creation survives and thrives. They have never forgotten that Earth is our home and we must care for it.

Can we find the wisdom to see that our future is bound up with the future of our planet? Can we gather the wisdom to see past our divisions and rediscover that we are all one creation as we move into the future?

In looking backward, I remembered the *concept of the common good* and it too became a "precious egg." This belief — so strong in Catholic social justice teaching — is in our political documents as well. But it seems many have lost and forgotten how to live for the common good.

Politically, it means a mutual commitment to the common goods that benefit society as a whole and the value of political action as public service. In Christianity the common good is rooted in compassion — 'do unto others what you would have them do unto you.'

Can this concept of the common good be brought to bear on freeing ourselves from an individualistic consumer culture, so that as a nation we can provide essential services ensuring that all basic human needs are satisfied as we move into the future?

Finally, I reflected on Pope Francis' challenge to the church as he builds upon the "precious eggs" of Vatican II and the tradition of Catholic social justice teaching; calling us to connect our faith journey with our role as citizens. In *Evangelii Gaudium*, "The Joy of the Gospel," Pope Francis wrote that "an authentic faith ... always involves a deep desire to change the world, to transmit values, to leave this earth somehow better than we found it. ... The earth is our common home and all of us are brothers and sisters. If indeed 'the just ordering of society and of the state is a central responsibility of politics,' the Church 'cannot and must not remain on the sidelines in the fight for justice.'"[65]

Can we embody an understanding of faith that deepens the Vatican II theology and its subsequent developments that we are in the world and not separate? Can we be part of a true communion that is constantly open to encounter, dialogue, attentive listening, and mutual assistance?

As we continue moving forward, we also take time to turn our heads backward and see what other wisdom emerges from our past. What are those "precious eggs" that we will need if we are to learn from our past and move forward together?

Let that wisdom sink in, and when we sit in contemplation simply let go — surrendering to the workings of Divine Love. We will then know where to go back and how to fetch the "precious eggs" for our future.

• Can Christians Be Progressive? Absolutely!

Judy Woodruff, in a segment on the PBS NewsHour, posed this question in a focus group of eight Republicans – 'Can a Christian or a person of deep faith be politically progressive?' Each answered "No."

Depending on how one understands progressive, I would answer absolutely!

Recently, I was involved with a project with Network, a national Catholic social justice lobby, where I served as executive director from 1982-1992. Mary Novak, the current executive director, invited me to design a contemplative listening process to assist congregations of women religious in reflecting on their legacy of social justice, and imagining how it can continue to evolve as religious life transforms.

The responses during the listening sessions stirred a renewed passion in my heart for what women religious have done as they lived into the mandate from the 1971 Synod of Bishops, which stated that "Action on behalf of justice is a constitutive dimension of the preaching of the Gospel." Those words were transformative for women religious. Together with the documents of the Second Vatican Council, women religious in the U.S. began to see their ministries through a new lens. Over these past 60 years, the work of social justice and systemic change has been central to the embodiment of the charism of religious life.

Those words took flesh as congregations reflected on the legacy of U.S. women religious, beautifully recorded by Mary Novak.

Listen to what they had to say about the source of their actions:

- Our action comes from the depth of our connection to the holy.

> *We must continue to evolve the ongoing mandate of action on behalf of justice as a constitutive dimension of preaching the Gospel into the future.*
>
> *Pope Francis challenges all people of good faith, deeply religious, Christian, or Catholic, to be multi-issue advocates, supporting political positions that foster the common good and address the needs of the many over the wants of the few.*

- It is deeply mystical and contemplative, stemming from the breadth and depth of our life in God.
- Prayer, relationship to the holy, as well as community, grounded us and opened us to find God in surprising places.
- It transformed us and helped to create church for so many and kept so many in the church.
- We took the Gospel seriously and embraced the commitment to human dignity.
- We kept our eyes and ears open to those who were not being served elsewhere, those who were being excluded, and those who were on the margins or the periphery, as Pope Francis likes to say.
- Our response was in relationship with others who were suffering and in need of healing and whose suffering broke open our hearts.
- Our response was in conversation with experience, recognizing the resilience of those with whom we had the privilege to walk.

This deep faith and commitment to the Gospel found expression in actions as they:

- Read the signs of the times and saw the evolving spectrum of their work from charity to justice to systemic change to transformation of consciousness.
- Recognized the importance of political ministry to change federal policies and ensure the common good by providing the basic human needs necessary to safeguard the dignity of every creature.
- Used their finances for socially responsible and impact investing, thereby challenging corporations to prioritize the health of Earth and its people over profits.
- Went to the margins, to the periphery, where those who suffer from structural injustice live, in order to speak truth in love rooted in experience.
- Used their voice in the public arena and took corporate stances.
- Understood the centrality of Earth and integrated sustainability and care of the Earth into their understanding of systemic change.
- Grew into the realization that we are all connected — sentient and non-sentient beings — and viewed issues and each other through this lens.
- Understood and named how they and all have been complicit in injustices perpetrated by white privilege, holding a both/and position as they sought forgiveness and offered reparations.

Understanding the Gospel in this way expands the work of justice in the public forum biased toward certain things:

- Biased toward the welfare and future of the planet, ensuring clean air, water, and other natural resources, therefore needing to address climate change.
- Biased toward those who are economically disadvantaged and lacking the basic needs of food, shelter, health care, and education.

- Biased toward those whose human dignity and equality are ignored.
- Biased toward a more equitable distribution of wealth, goods, and services within an economic system that still values individual profit over the common good.
- Biased toward an international community in which peace and justice prevail and people are welcomed across borders.

To take seriously the Gospel mandate "to love one another as oneself," challenges all Christians to expand the focus of their political positions. Too often, a singular focus on issues of sexuality defines a Christian's political stance. Pope Francis challenges all people of good faith, deeply religious, Christian, or Catholic, to be multi-issue advocates, supporting political positions that foster the common good and address the needs of the many over the wants of the few.

Legislation that embodies those positions is considered progressive and was supported by both political parties in the past. It is only recently that the word 'progressive' has become central in today's war of words. The extreme right paints those with whom they disagree with the broad brush stroke of progressive, describing it with the words communist, liberal, socialist, fascist, etc. which generate fear for many.

The vast majority of women religious throughout these last decades have shown that embodying the mandate of love within the public arena is to support policies that embrace the needs of the poorest throughout the world as well as protecting our Earth home. It is supporting issues and public policies which are often categorized as a progressive agenda. We cannot let the work of love be sabotaged by an extreme minority dismissing these efforts as un-Christian. I feel the time we are in challenges both women religious and others who have followed a similar path to be prepared to engage in conversation about why we believe what we support from a stance of love. That is key.

Today's political climate challenges us to move away from an either-or position and embrace a both-and posture. In our democracy, we need to take positions on specific legislation and elect those who support those policies. AND rooted in our love for one another, we need to open ourselves to listen to each other, to engage in conversation about differences, to be open to other possibilities so that we begin to heal and lessen the divisions among us.

For me, that is what contemplation invites us into now. We are invited to continue deepening our contemplative gaze, 'to take a long loving look at the real,' and to interpret the times not only through analysis but through the eye of the heart. This will help create a spaciousness to awaken to God, Divine Mystery, within us so that we can respond out of a new consciousness, Christ consciousness. We must continue to evolve the ongoing mandate of action on behalf of justice as a constitutive dimension of preaching the Gospel into the future.

SPACIOUSNESS TO CREATE

Take time to breathe and enter the spaciousness of your heart.

For a period of time, sit in contemplation, setting the intention to be open to Divine Love within you. With your contemplative gaze, reflect on your experience in Gallery Four. Was anything evoked in you, became present to you, challenged, or shifted in you? Bring expression to it creatively through words, drawing, poetry, doodle, or ...

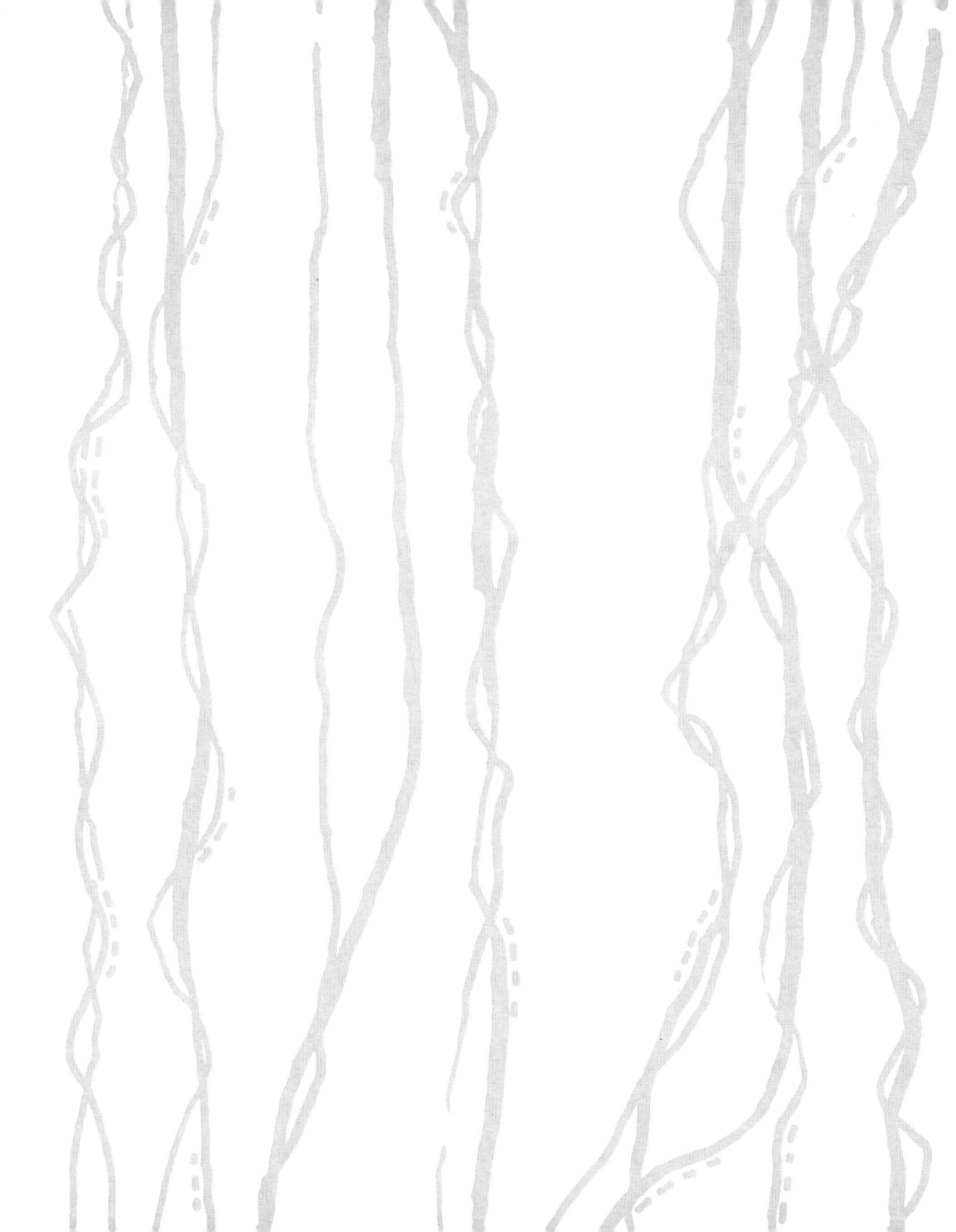

Gallery 5:

CHRISTIAN FEASTS

In this gallery, the reflections draw insights from current theology and science to offer renewed meaning to these powerful mysteries within the Christian tradition that are part of the Liturgical Cycle.

Each celebration, some lasting a day and some weeks, reminds us throughout the year of the significant mysteries of faith in the life of Jesus. They serve as touchstones inviting us to deepen our understanding and experience of Divine Mystery. Unfortunately, they often become simply repetitive events. The Mystery and beauty of what is being conveyed needs to be reawakened.

- **Advent**
- **Christmas**
- **Epiphany**
- **Lent**
- **Ash Wednesday**
- **Triduum**
    - **Holy Thursday**
    - **Good Friday**
    - **Holy Saturday**
- **Easter**

• Advent

It seems public preparations for Christmas are beginning earlier and earlier, and what is becoming more overlooked is the season of Advent. It is a quieter time, a time of waiting; a time to prepare oneself. Advent invites us to reflect on the historical birth of Jesus and the future yet to be of the Second Coming. Advent is a time of hope.

Given the world we live in, "hope" is certainly needed. We are surrounded by violence among nations and within nations, hunger and famine, dislocation of millions of people now worldwide refugees in search of a new home. The anger and negative rhetoric that fills the airwaves creates a sensation that that is all there is. Why wouldn't you imagine the future reflecting such a Dystopian perspective when there is such great suffering and injustice?

And yet, Advent is a season of hope celebrating a historical moment and a yet-to-be cosmic event. Advent invites us to reflect on the insights of our ancestors in faith and continue to deepen that experience freeing us to encounter anew the gifts of the Incarnation and the Second Coming.

The scripture readings in Advent are filled with the prophet Isaiah's hopeful future vision, beautifully expressed in images and words that stir our hearts with possibility. We hear: "They shall beat their swords into plowshares and their spears into pruning hooks ... one nation shall not raise the sword against another, nor shall they train for war again." (Isaiah 2:4) and "justice shall be the band around his waist, and faithfulness a belt upon his hips ... the wolf shall be a guest of the lamb and the leopard shall lie down with the kid; the calf and the young lion shall browse together, with a little child to guide them." (Isaiah 11:6). Psalm 85 poetically captures that vision: "Kindness and truth shall meet; Justice and Peace shall kiss."

> **Advent invites us to reflect on the insights of our ancestors in faith and continue to deepen that experience freeing us to encounter anew the gifts of the Incarnation and the Second Coming.**
>
> **We shall never know all that the Incarnation still expects of the world's potentialities.**

For the Hebrew community, Jesus embodied that vision. He became God's love incarnate. There was an understanding that the Divine and the human were connected, that God was personal and intimate, as well as transcendent and omnipotent. Decades after Jesus' death the priests and scholars would debate how this could be and over time they articulated within the philosophical and theological framework of their historical time that Jesus was both human and divine.

The religious imagination offered us a glimpse of that intimate, loving God in the Gospel accounts of Jesus' birth. We are brought into the birthing room where Mary delivers the infant Jesus to the world. We can sense his vulnerability, his innocence, his beauty. He grows up in ways that amplify the hope of the prophets as reflected in the parables, sermons, and miracles found in the Gospels. We even witness Jesus' suffering and death on the cross. Unjustly accused we sense the agony of a mother, friends, and followers. Jesus, Divine Love incarnate, has lived and died.

The situation seemed pretty dire after Jesus' death and yet there was an impulse, a mystical knowing that Divine Love was still present and in fact would come in fullness at the end of time with the Second Coming.

Today, over 2000 years later, we continue to remember the birth of the historical Jesus and celebrate it at Christmas. However, the very world in which Jesus lived we now understand in new ways thanks to the James Webb telescope, the insights into evolution, quantum physics, the development of consciousness, and other physical and social sciences. These insights reveal to us that we are all interconnected across space and time. Evolution continues and this next emergence is dependent on our consciousness, a consciousness that for Christians is putting on the mind of Christ or Christ consciousness and that what each of us chooses to do affects the future. The Incarnation of Divine Love continues through us, and the Second Coming depends on us continuing to live the prophetic vision fulfilled in Jesus. The "hope" of the future is emerging as we remember Jesus' life and choose to live accordingly.

Teilhard de Chardin, SJ, understood the implications of these scientific shifts in relation to our faith.[66] He also understood the suffering and horror of war having been a stretcher bearer in WWI. His writing poetically gives voice to a renewed understanding of Incarnation and the Second Coming, to the experience of the vastness and intimacy of God, and to the hope that is calling us from the future. Teilhard[67] writes:

> *God is the atmosphere in which we are bathed. God encompasses us on all sides, like the world itself. What prevents you, then, from enfolding God in your arms? (Divine Milieu)*
>
> *We shall never know all that the Incarnation still expects of the world's potentialities. (Divine Milieu)*

As the transformation follows its natural line of progress we can foresee the time when humanity will understand what it is, animated by one single heart, to be united together in wanting, hoping for, and loving the same things at the sametime. The humankind of tomorrow is emerging from the mists of the future, and we can actually see it taking shape: a superhumankind, much more conscious, much more powerful, and much more unanimous than our own. (Toward the Future)

Advent affords us the time to remember the birth of the historical Jesus and to remember his life as showing us how to live. In that memory is hope, a hope that finds its fulfillment in the yet to be cosmic event—the Second Coming. A poster of Corita Kent captures this anticipation: 'Hope is the memory of the future ... have a hand in creating it.'[68]

This Advent season take some time to ponder both the Incarnation and the Second Coming through the lens of these words. Let them stir your heart. Then deepen them through your contemplative practice. Our future is in need of us. May we all have a hand in creating it.

• Christmas

If we ever needed the Incarnation, we need it today. Something seems to be infecting us as a people. There seems to be a blindness and a deafness to see and hear each other as we truly are and to understand our place within the whole Earth community. There is a destructive energy among us that feeds our fears. It preys on our differences. It asserts that for us to be secure we need to keep others separate from us. Because we can't see or hear, we are stuck right where we are; and no facts, moral persuasion, or even personal experience of another's suffering can move us.

This toxic atmosphere belies our belief in the Incarnation, which reveals to us that God, by whatever name, is one with humanity and creation. Jesus gave God flesh, blood, and a body and told us we are all loved and we need to love one another. We are all one. Our faith will fail us if we do not allow this mystery to penetrate our hearts in ways that call forth from us a more mature faith.

Today we are learning so much about our world and our place in it through evolution, quantum physics, and the breakthroughs in cosmology. I find myself wondering if there is an invitation in all of this to exercise and stretch our religious imagination as we contemplate the Incarnation.

Scientists teach us that the universe began 13.8 billion years ago in a great flaring forth of a dense singularity of energy. From that explosion evolved time, space, and what is called the *vacuum* — a sea of potentiality from within which everything arises as fluctuations of its energy. It is full of life. Everything that exists was present at that first flaring forth. And it has been evolving ever since.

Pierre Teilhard de Chardin, SJ, saw evolution as a movement toward more complexity. He stated that the only real evolution is that of convergence because it is positive and creative. For Teilhard evolution has a directionality toward greater complexity and wholeness.[69]

> *In a flash of one life, God consciousness broke through to a new stage in the evolutionary process.*
>
> *Stretching our religious imagination can be fun, but it is also very challenging for it breaks open new ways of being and doing.*

We are also coming to understand that cooperation is essential to survival. At significant points in the evolutionary process, it was the convergence or cooperation between or among elements that formed something new. Evolution is marked by increasing wholeness in nature. As we have come from the same source we are evolving into the fullness of the Omega point, or in Teilhard's words, Christogenesis.

Energy has a central role as we are learning that the material universe is fundamentally energy. There are different forms of energy but all of life is charged with energy. Quantum physics tells us that a particle split in two can communicate over vast distances. Rupert Sheldrake posits the concept of a morphogenetic field that carries information from one generation to another making it easier for its replication in future generations.[70] As more and more of us begin to do something it becomes easier for others to learn it.

Such insights offer a new space within our religious imagination to play, to stretch, and to see if there are ways to complement the Christmas Nativity scene, the gift of St. Francis' imagination. Let us imagine Divine Love Incarnate made visible in an evolving universe's journey toward wholeness.

What if we imagine . . .

God as Divine source, Divine energy, the *vacuum* present throughout the evolutionary process. God manifesting God's self in the emergence of galaxies, earth, life, consciousness, and us.

Then rather than feeling this cosmic story to be cold, abstract, and distant, it becomes personal, part of our genealogy, part of our own emergence. And we share this history with Jesus whose intimacy with his Abba God witnesses to the unimaginable significance of every single life.

People who experienced Jesus knew him to be different than other teachers of his day. He preached a message of radical inclusivity. He welcomed the outcasts, the sinners. He spoke to women and included them as disciples. He healed the suffering and the sick. He gathered his friends as a community of equals. He told us to love one another as ourselves. He warned us that if we see a splinter in someone's eye to look for the beam in our own. He related to all with compassion and mercy. He taught that we are all one, like his Abba God and he were one. He promised that his Abba God would dwell within each of us. His energy went out of him inviting people to come and see and then to follow. He was seen as authentic and lived what he believed to the fullest even when it alienated the powers that be. His followers witnessed him willing to suffer and die rather than betray what he believed to be the living out of his Abba God's will.

In a flash of one life, God consciousness broke through to a new stage in the evolutionary process. Jesus accessed the fullness of divinity at a historical moment that was open to this emergence.

What if Jesus holds the potentiality for everyone to access their God self?

What if we imagine the Incarnation as an invitation to celebrate the potentiality that is ours if we open ourselves in contemplation 'to take a long loving look at the real?' To try to see ourselves as more alike than different with all whom inhabit this planet. Imagine us moving together as an Earth community to greater wholeness, seeking the common good, understanding everyone and everything is sacred. To be open enough to see the beam in my own eye so as not to judge the splinter in the eye of the other.

What if we see ourselves as the followers of Jesus being part of a morphogenetic field? In the mystical body of Christ, we have been evolving, learning throughout time how to be more like Jesus. What if the incarnation continues in you and me, in the evolutionary process? What if the process invites us to manifest God consciousness as Jesus showed us *here and now* so as to affect the evolutionary process toward wholeness?

Stretching our religious imagination can be fun, but it is also very challenging for it breaks open new ways of being and doing.

This Christmas you might want to play with reimagining this mystery. When you think about the shepherds looking at the sky, reflect for a moment on how the universe began. Gaze at the stars, the galaxies, and the immensity of it all. The shepherds knew something great was happening. What do you sense? Can you imagine God's presence in a radically new way? You may just find yourself breaking out into songs of praise like the angels or becoming awe-struck. Think about the family we call holy. Imagine how important every individual is and how each of us needs the other to discover our true selves. Imagine how they must have lived sensing the presence of God in their lives and being open to seeing it in new ways to make choices that furthered the evolutionary process toward fullness.

We contemplate that in Jesus Divinity and Humanity are one. For some, it is incomprehensible that this could happen with a simple carpenter's son. For some, it is even a scandal. Yet it is the profound gift of Incarnation — the realization that we are all children of God invited to share in the Divine Consciousness. Our planet needs us to accept incarnation and live it.

This Christmas I am going to imagine giving that gift to everyone, sending forth the energy of our oneness. Perhaps you will join me. May you have a very merry reimagined Christmas!

• Epiphany

John Philip Newell in quoting Eriugena[71] in his book *Sacred Earth, Sacred Soul*, says that everything is sacred, but we live in a state of forgetfulness about what is deepest in us.[72] The more we forget our true identity, the less we treat one another as sacred. We suffer from "soul-forgetfulness."

The celebration of Epiphany wakes us up. We become conscious of something very important. We remember the person Jesus, who as Eriugena says, comes to show us what we have forgotten: that we are bearers of the divine flow. Jesus reawakens us to our true nature and creation's true nature: that we are all sacred.

As we become more aware of who we are as Incarnation "coming into being" we will radiate that outward. We will act and be in new ways and it will nourish those around us and beyond. One of the profound gifts of Incarnation is that we are all invited to share in divine consciousness. The immensity and complexity of the world in which we live can be overwhelming. Yet, the invitation is there for each of us to become who we are at our essence, our core. Each of us has something to give to the entirety of the world. Our planet needs us to accept that gift and live it.

The future will continue to call us forth but the choice of which direction we go is ours. Like the three wise ones who trusted the star to find where they were going and their dream telling them to return a different way, we will have many choices to make in the months and years ahead. An awakened sense of who we are is needed to respond now and in this world.

Contemplative practice can awaken us to that gift and deepen our desire to open it, freeing us to engage all that distracts us and keeps us from seeing who we are. When we

> *The more we forget our true identity, the less we treat one another as sacred. We suffer from 'soul-forgetfulness.'*
>
> *The future will continue to call us forth but the choice of which direction we go is ours. An awakened sense of who we are is needed to respond now and in this world.*

do choose to open that gift, we are invited to live out of Christ consciousness as you and me. It is to embody the good news Jesus preached over 2,000 years ago. It is to offer our unique self to the world. Our source is Divine Loving — intimate and unending. Each of us in our uniqueness is essential to the present and emerging future.

Take some time to "sit" — to rest in Divine Love and be open to the "you" who is emerging. Let the words of Jan Richardson in her blessing "For Those Who Have Far to Travel: An Epiphany Blessing" companion you:

> *If you could see*
> *the journey whole,*
> *You might never*
> *undertake it,*
> *Might never dare*
> *the first step*
> *That propels you*
> *from the place*
> *You have known*
> *toward the place*
> *You know not.*[73]

And then recommit to the vision that is calling you forth.

• Lent

Liturgically, the Lenten season takes us on a journey. The story of Jesus' public life is told once again. Like us, Jesus lived in a tumultuous time. There were divisions within the political and religious groups. People were sick and in need of healing. Certain types of people were considered outcasts as defined by a strict purity code and shunned by most. There were entitled groups among the religious leaders who flaunted privileges that oppressed others. It was in this milieu that Jesus entered his public ministry.

In Jesus, we witness a man who responded to the injustices of his time out of love and not fear and without blame in ways that reflected a different worldview, a different consciousness. He saw all as equal and not divided by the purity code of his time. He welcomed the unclean to join him. He healed those who couldn't see physically but could "see" the power that Jesus offered them when he would ask, "And what do you want me to do for you?" He proclaimed his truth even though it would incite the ecclesial and political authorities. He loved and forgave those who could not accept his words and his invitations. He was tortured, accused of a crime he did not commit, and he suffered the death penalty of the time — crucifixion. He even cried out in desperation, seeking God whom he felt abandoned him.

At the end of his life, Jesus had nothing to show for it. Most of his followers abandoned or denied him or hid lest they be seen as associates of his. Only the women stayed and were among the first to encounter the mystery of resurrected life.

The Gospels also tell us that Jesus often prayed: intensely for forty days alone, after giving of himself serving people's needs, after exercising his power, and communally at meals.

> *Jesus ...*
> *responded to the*
> *injustices of his time*
> *out of love*
> *and not fear ...*
>
> *Jesus' prayer went*
> *beyond words,*
> *beyond thinking,*
> *resting in Divine Love*
> *but not a resting*
> *of inaction; rather,*
> *resting freed him from*
> *current ways of thinking*
> *so he could 'see'*
> *in new ways.*

His prayer went beyond words, beyond thinking. Jesus rested in Divine Love but not a resting of inaction. Rather, resting freed him from current ways of thinking and opened a spaciousness within him so that he could "see" in new ways. Jesus' heart became his organ of perception responding from the indwelling of Divine Love to be in service to all.

The magnetic center of Divine Love dwells within each of us — drawing us, inviting us to make the space for us to "see" in new ways and to respond from that love.

When we set the intention to access the Divine dwelling within ourselves and acknowledge that desire in every person it readies us to listen and speak to each other in new ways. It opens up a space where we begin to imagine new responses to people, issues, and problems. Over time we begin to see the Godself in the other. We realize that we have all come from the same star dust as cosmologists are telling us. We begin to understand that we all breathe the same air and receive nourishment from the same water. We know deep in our bones that we are all connected. And when we do, we cannot demonize the other anymore.

This Lent, let us open a spaciousness within ourselves 'to take a long loving look at the real' of our time and be aware of the journey that is ours as we live out of our magnetic center of Divine Love.

• Ash Wednesday

We read in John's Gospel that "God so loved the world that God gave God's only son to save the world." That is often given as the reason for the presence of Jesus in our midst. But what if there is more?

"There is something more than just a rescue operation going on here; the created world is infinitely precious and valuable in its own right," writes Cynthia Bourgeault in *The Holy Trinity and the Law of Three*.[74]

This world is the Earth upon which we live and to which we return as our "dust to dust" mantra reminds us every Ash Wednesday when we are blessed with ashes and hear "Remember, you are dust and to dust you shall return." We come from matter and this material world holds Divinity. Jesus didn't become less when he was born. Divinity didn't get diminished when incarnated into matter. Our binary way of thinking that one must be better than the other — divinity/humanity, spirit/matter — doesn't work here. We are being turned around, invited to see things differently. The way to God is not "up" in an ascending manner but more "down" in a descent.

Bourgeault is helpful again: "by entering the realm of form ... descent seems to be the chief operative in making the fullness of the divine manifestation happen."[75] The world we live in is holy, and matter is a most appropriate container for Divine Love.

Jesus emptied himself into life fully and lovingly. As the Scripture stories tell us, he looked at everyone as worthy of encounter, from the lepers exiled in caves to the prostituted women of his time. The sick, the maimed, the deaf and mute he called to be in relationship with him, to share the healing power of love, forgiveness, and mercy. All those who chose to follow him were invited to see things differently and to wake up to what was really there.

> *Jesus' presence in our midst is more than a rescue operation for the world.*
>
> *The world we live in is holy, and matter was a most appropriate container for Divine Love.*

Those in positions of power and privilege during Jesus' time felt threatened with Jesus' lifestyle. What would happen if everyone was seen as equal, worthy of respect and dignity from one another? What would happen if the high priests couldn't define which sacrifices, rules, and laws were necessary to follow if people wanted to achieve a higher place in heaven? What if more people believed Jesus' message that God lives within us all?

Lent reveals the answer. The power of Love is so great a force that if not stopped — put to death — it would transform the world. The systems, structures, and consciousness that privilege the few over the many would be no more.

Jesus' act of self-emptying love ended in death. His entire life was an act of love — exchanging, giving, and receiving. But his death was not an isolated act, no matter how meaningless it may have appeared to those who stood at the foot of the cross.

During Lent, we re-awaken to the gift of love as embodied in the life of Jesus. It is our acts of compassion, mercy, and self-emptying love that not only transform our behavior but our very being, and consequently, the world. And that transformation is what threatens those in power.

Bourgeault expresses it best as she writes in *The Wisdom Jesus*: "Something is catalyzed out of that self-emptying which is pure divine substance mirrored in our own true face. Subtle qualities of divine love essential to the well-being of this planet are released through our actions and flow out into the world as miracle, healing, and hope."[76]

This year when you hear, "Remember you are dust and to dust you will return," celebrate that you (we) are part of Earth, matter through which Divinity manifests itself. As you are marked with the sign of the cross, remember that you (we) are human beings who are invited to join the divine dance of outpouring love here on this Earth.

• Triduum

Jesus lived out of a highly evolved consciousness that enters into us, and is, over time changing our hearts and the way we view the world. But we are not there yet. I found Thomas Keating's words very helpful in extending compassion to those with whom I am so dismayed. He agrees that humanity seems stuck in the evolutionary process. He writes in *Reflections on the Unknowable:* "We are literally crucified between heaven and earth. When you look at a cross, even though nobody's on it, you see a marvelous symbol of where the human condition is right now. To get out of that place requires an integration of joy and sorrow, of hope and knowledge of our weakness."[77]

We are all part of humanity. We are all crucified between heaven and earth. We are all invited to admit our weaknesses and our selfishness. We are all invited to grow beyond ourselves to embrace the reality that we are all connected. In the Catholic tradition, we know that as the Mystical Body of Christ, we are one body and we need each other.

The unity of the human family, the whole planetary community, is the Good News of this Easter season. It is what Jesus proclaimed by his life, death, and resurrection.

> *We are all invited to grow beyond ourselves to embrace the reality that we are all connected.*

• Holy Thursday

As the Triduum begins I find myself pondering Jesus' invitation to us to shift perspective. Beatrice Bruteau makes this come alive in her book, *The Holy Thursday Revolution.*[78] She reminds us that Jesus was a boundary-breaker. He broke the boundary of the purity system that divided people into clean and unclean. The parable of the Good Samaritan exemplified this when the despised and unclean Samaritan turned out to be the hero. He broke the boundary of family; letting us know that it is not family lineage that counts but rather hearing the word of God and living it. He broke the boundary between people who are rich and poor, as well as diseased and healthy. He broke the boundary between women and men, treating them exactly alike. Finally, he broke the boundary between friends and enemies, understanding that God sends the sun and rain on good and evil individuals alike.

Bruteau also reflects on the profound act of Jesus washing the disciples' feet on the night before he died. That gesture of the master acting like a servant proclaims his vision that we are all equal and turns the way the world works upside down. That act is disorienting and disruptive. She reminds us that the disciples are shocked. Peter is the one who objects. He was afraid because if he consented to this action, then everything would change and things could not go back to the way they were. Everything would have to be readjusted — relationships, values and attitudes. In that revolutionary act a new consciousness emerged among Jesus' followers.

Jesus invites us to see things through that new consciousness. He tells us that we are all friends and that the power of God is in us to do as he has done, and even more. He tells us that God lives in him and he in God. That God is in each of us and each of us is in God. It is a dance of mutuality and relationships. Equality, mutuality, abundance, non-violence, and interconnectedness are lenses through which Jesus sees the world.

> *Equality, mutuality, abundance, non-violence, and interconnectedness are lenses through which Jesus sees the world.*

When we celebrate the Eucharist today, remember we are becoming part of the larger community in a more intimate way. Whether we are fully aware of it or not, we are saying that we are willing to grow into the person God desires us to be. We are setting ourselves on a path toward "wholeness" or holiness which will invite us to embrace the brutal realities that are part of our world and the remnants of violence that live within us. We are committing ourselves to live in communion with all life; which is to live in solidarity with the oppressed, excluded, and exploited, and to help sustain our Earth home.

• Good Friday

An image has haunted me since I first read it in an article about the atrocities taking place in South Sudan. It is very disturbing, and I'd rather move past it quickly, acknowledging this happens but not dwelling on it. However, as I read it, the image of Jesus on the cross appeared in my mind's eye and became a scrim through which I cannot help but continue to reflect on the image.

As in so many war-torn countries, rape has proliferated in South Sudan. The article spoke of "survivors turning up in refugee camps giving harrowing accounts of women being tied against trees and gang-raped by armed combatants from both sides of the conflict."

As I let that sink in, I am filled with tears and outrage. The image is so stark, and it cuts deep as I reflect on being a woman and how vulnerable my body is to those who see it as a spoil of war; who see it as an object that can be used and abused to satisfy some sick release of the sexual urge; or who can only be sexually satisfied by violent conquest.

We know South Sudan is not the only place where such crucifixions occur. It happens in countries not at war; it happens in cities; it happens in homes. Women and the life-giving power of our bodies continue to threaten men who do not understand mutuality and the beauty of sexuality rooted in love.

Something happens in war or wherever men are given weapons and permission to kill. That kind of power must feed our reptilian brain in ways that we have yet to understand. Despite our ignorance, however, we continue feeding wars with national budgets that provide billions for the military, by lining the pockets of private companies through arms sales, and by choosing violence over diplomacy to bring an end to conflicts. Who loses in such choices? In South Sudan, it is the women and children. In our planetary community, it is all of us.

> *Women tied against trees and gang-raped ....*
> *Jesus on the cross became visible again.*
> *Tears streamed down his face.*
> *He couldn't 'fix it.'*
> *It is as if*
> *in his surrender,*
> *in the absence of any guarantee that things would work out,*
> *redemption happened.*

Women tied against trees and gang-raped.

As I read those words, the image of Jesus on the cross became visible. It was as if he could feel what was happening and wept again, suffered again. He lived his life the only way he knew how. He loved. He spoke as friends to those whom his culture, his society, and his religion rejected. He had a vision that could include everyone and which could forgive. He got angry but he didn't hurt and he didn't maim and he didn't rape to prove his manhood. He didn't do anything to deserve such an ignominious death.

I imagine these women going about their day in the only way they knew how. Trying to keep their children safe from the ravages of war. Doing whatever they could to find food in a country where 100,000 people face famine. Caring for their sick as they face a cholera outbreak. Praying that their children would not be conscripted into the fighting as more than 17,000 child soldiers already have. They didn't do anything to deserve such violence that too often led to their death.

I imagined that Jesus' head was down and tears streamed from his face. He couldn't "fix it." Not then and not now. It is as if in his surrender, in the absence of any guarantee that things would work out, redemption happened. Jesus trusted despite any evidence that transformation was happening.

I see the women of South Sudan, women everywhere, who have been brutalized and crucified, upon their crosses surrounding Jesus. Together their sufferings and deaths keep the heavens open raining down the grace, the energy, and the love needed for our future transformation.

• Holy Saturday

Holy Saturday always felt 'empty' to me. Liturgically after the Good Friday service the altar is stripped bare, and the Eucharistic presence is removed and placed on a side altar. That symbolizes the time between Jesus' burial and his Resurrection. The time when Jesus descended into hell or in some translations 'stormed the gates of hell'. Nothing happens that day. No liturgy is celebrated until midnight when the Easter Vigil begins.

In the tradition of 'storming the gates of hell,' I invite you to lament, to give passionate expression to your grief and sorrow at what is happening in the world. You may want to pray the lament that follows out loud. Or you may want to write something yourself or simply find a private space to loudly express your pain.

Why? Oh, God are millions of people torn away from their homes, exiled to other lands, their places of shelter destroyed, and the land wasted?

> Why are mothers and children separated from the people they love who are off fighting neighbors as in the days of old?

> My God, have we not learned anything?

Where are You, Holy Wisdom, present through the ages, where are you now when decision-makers are faced with excruciating choices as to how to defend an unjust invasion now that there is a nuclear option?

> How did we arm ourselves in ways that escalate violence rather than protect us from unjust assaults?

> Holy Wisdom, where are you when we need to imagine new possibilities for peace?

Divine Compassion, where are you when economic sanctions are used to stop war and we see only inflation as prices increase at the gas pump?

**Lament, give passionate expression to your grief and sorrow at what is happening in the world ...
May the hope of new life amid such suffering be given to us all.**

How did we become so tolerant of our capacity to consume that we are blinded to the basic human needs of so many throughout the world?

Divine Compassion, have you abandoned us as we serve our own needs and desires first?

Holy and Loving One, what is happening to our world seemingly gone mad?

Where are you when we are facing chaos and must imagine new ways forward?

Where are you when all that we took for granted is shifting before our eyes?

Where are you when we need to know that Love continues to hold us together and that we all are one?

Jesus on the cross cried out, "My God, my God, why have you forsaken me?" With that lament, he freed himself to experience the unimaginable possibility of life after death. May the hope of new life amid such suffering be given to us all.

• Easter

Early, before dawn, I awakened consumed with worry and fear about the future. I couldn't fall back to sleep as I tried to reconstruct the dream that awakened me and which I was sure held an answer if I could only remember. The past few days I had noticed a growing resistance to situations, people, and ideas that I've responded to in the past with compassion and understanding. Now I found myself reacting, annoyed with everyone and everything. I found myself alone anticipating an impending storm without any sense of direction.

Many people speak of having such experiences of being alone and feeling alone, feeling abandoned in the face of the death of spouses, siblings, children, friends, and colleagues. Consumed by anxiety, overwhelmed in facing a future that is uncertain and not at all what was hoped for or imagined, these feelings can lead to depression, addiction, and, in the extreme, suicide. All of which have been on the rise in recent years. In the past, formal religions offered comfort and guidance in these situations; but with more and more people leaving traditional religious institutions, that is often no longer the case.

The separation between religion and science begun in the 1400's has widened over the centuries. Some people retained belief in what has always been taught in the churches, rejecting evolution and other insights of science that might have informed their faith. Many others saw religion as irrelevant to address the complex world of today, with its scientific and technological breakthroughs.

The Covid pandemic revealed the underside of many institutions and systems that we have relied on over these last centuries, many of which are failing us and cannot bring us into the future. To paraphrase the quote attributed to Albert Einstein, we cannot solve the problems of today out of the same level of consciousness that created them.

> *We can draw strength from Jesus here and now to live lives with the fullness of eternity if we remember that even after death our personhood remains alive "hidden with Christ in God."*

The existential questions that are arising in us need to be responded to out of a new vision. Who am I in this world? Am I alone or are we connected? Is there meaning in life? Does what I do make a difference? Is this universe a vast empty space void of any purpose? What happens after I die?

Today, these questions and the experiences that gave rise to them will not be addressed out of a past consciousness; rather the future consciousness will need to envision a both/and relationship between faith and science.

I don't think it was an accident that my "awakening" happened in Holy Week. I found myself, as I often do, drawn to the final discourse in John's Gospel (Chapters 14-17). There Jesus tells his friends, "Do not let your hearts be troubled; I'm going to prepare a place for you; I will not leave you orphans; you all are one; you will do greater things than I and you are to love one another."

The existential questions were being addressed. I found myself returning to my Christian faith, not simply as I learned it growing up, but rather as informed by ancient wisdom traditions, interfaith perspectives, and especially the insights of evolution and quantum physics to calm my fears and offer insights into moving forward.

Quantum physics is turning the classical scientific worldview upside down. The rational, linear, atomized, mechanistic worldview that shaped so many of our modern institutions/systems has run its course. Faced now with a greater sense of alienation and fragmentation, humanity knows at a deep level that there is something more.

What we are learning is that everything is connected at all levels of existence. Reality has many dimensions — most of which cannot be observed or measured. Consciousness is central to reality, and the human person is a participant in the evolutionary process. There are ways of knowing, other than the rational, that are needed to grasp what is being revealed and documented.

These current discoveries lend themselves to an openness to explore the spiritual dimensions of ourselves and our reality. The insights of quantum physics offer a new framework to express the religious impulse within us. It offers us a way of interpreting anew religious beliefs that touch into another way of knowing — of sensing what is — that have been lost these past centuries.

Cynthia Bourgeault explores these connections in her book, *Eye of the Heart*.[79] She discusses the dimensions of reality as different but connected realms of various energetic densities. She draws on the ancient wisdom traditions and Christian beliefs to describe an aliveness interpenetrating our earth and connecting it to the deeper infinite sources of creativity and abundance on a cosmic scale. These realms exist within a web of mutual nurturance. Each realm gives and receives from the other. This energetic exchange holds the whole created order together.

Perhaps another way of saying that is how Christian mystics proclaim that the entire Universe is permeated with the presence of Christ. The entire cosmos has become his body and the blood flowing through it is his love.[80] Jesus spent his life becoming more attuned to receive the intense spiritual energy necessary for his transformation. Through Jesus' death and resurrection, he showed us that the walls between the realms are paper thin interpenetrating and mutually permeable by love. We can draw strength from him here and now to live lives with the fullness of eternity if we remember that even after death our personhood remains alive "hidden with Christ in God."[81]

Such articulations stir my soul as new expressions of God's creation, everlasting life, life's purpose, and implications for our role in the whole enterprise.

We know we are not alone. We share a common earthly realm and are connected to other, more subtle realms through which we experience Divine creativity and abundance. We will encounter storms and pain, as they are part of the human condition. But we will not be held captive by that pain, for we are released through Jesus' willingness to live and die aligned with Divine Love. And Jesus assured us that we can live that way as well. Our choices do matter.

I may still be awakened worrying about my future not going according to my plans, but the invitation is there to trust, to let go — deeply aligning with Divine Love which permeates and embraces the many realms in which we live and breathe and have our being. That certainly is Easter Joy!

SPACIOUSNESS TO CREATE

Take time to breathe and enter the spaciousness of your heart.

For a period of time, sit in contemplation, setting the intention to be open to Divine Love within you. With your contemplative gaze, reflect on your experience in Gallery Five. Was anything evoked in you, became present to you, challenged, or shifted in you? Bring expression to it creatively through words, drawing, poetry, doodle, or ...

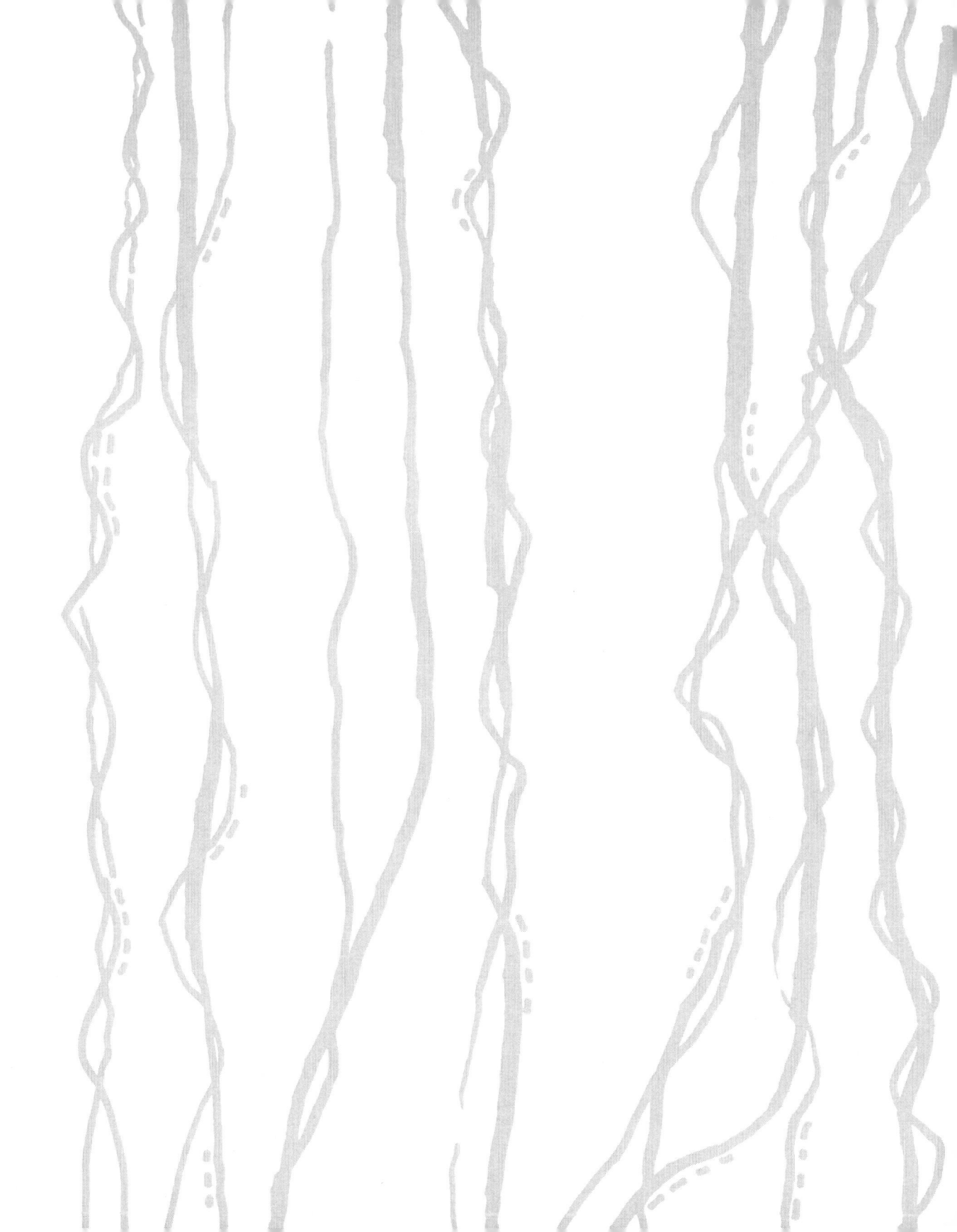

Gallery 6:

NATURE'S INSPIRATION

This gallery room is full of light. The windows invite the outside in to offer us the wisdom of nature. The cycle of life, death, and rebirth are always seeping in reminding us of what we have, what we must give up, and where we can find hope. The reflections in this gallery arise from experiences of the seasons in the bioregions of the upper Midwestern portion of the United States. You may want to consider the interplay of light and seasons in your bioregion.

- **Summer**

- **Fall**

- **Winter**

- **Spring**

• Summer

It is one of those perfect Michigan summer mornings; the temperature is in the high 70s, low humidity, the sun shining and the flowers fully blooming in all their rich colors. One of the sisters with whom I live is our gardener, and she has created a most splendid banquet of myriad flowers whose colors were profuse this morning.

As I stared at the flowers and became lost in the colors, I wondered what it would be like to be blind. What it would be to never have seen the great diversity and richness of flowers or the squirrels that scamper and play all day or the sights of city streets or the beauty of the lakes and oceans or the exquisite uniqueness of each other as we go about our lives.

As I prayed I realized that physical sight does not ensure seeing all that is there. No wonder contemplation is 'taking a long loving look at the real.' We need to create the space in us to see more broadly and deeply than a cursory look provides.

Of course, what we see is limited by what our consciousness allows us to see. The values, assumptions, and worldviews that are operative in our personal life as well as in the culture within which we live, the faith tradition we profess, and the economic class we identify with provide the lenses through which we view the world. Contemplation opens us to broaden those lenses; and to develop our consciousness so that we can see with greater complexity and inclusivity.

As I try to take that long loving look at what is happening in our world, I realize that what we tell ourselves about what we see — the story or the narrative out of which we act — is crucial. The old story no longer works, and the new story is only emerging. I believe we are living between a story of separation and a story of communion.

> *We are living between a story of separation and a story of communion.*

We keep telling a story rooted in a modern worldview. It is a story that tells us we are separate. Each person must look out for him/herself. There is not enough for everyone. There will be winners and losers. It keeps us from seeing beyond our own needs and wants.

We need to tell the other story, a story of communion — of seeing and welcoming the other — of belonging to each other not only to other human persons but to all beings.

As I was reflecting on being blind, I recalled one of my favorite Gospel stories. It is the story of Bartimaeus. He was physically blind, and when he encountered Jesus, Jesus asked Bartimaeus what he wanted him to do for him. Bartimaeus replied, "That I may see," and Jesus restored his sight. I don't think Jesus was making a statement that physical seeing makes someone better; rather, I believe Jesus wanted to teach us that we all need to see in new ways. Jesus' life made it clear that his worldview held that all were equal. All persons, regardless of how they ranked in the very strict purity code of his time, were embraced by him. Jesus spoke of communion and welcomed everyone to eat at his table. He lived out of abundance and not scarcity and saw the natural world as the world in which God's kindom would come.

That worldview, that consciousness, is needed today. I believe it is deep within us waiting to be awakened. It is what we see when we 'take a long loving look at the real.' It is the basis for the story of communion.

It is only softening our eyes and opening our hearts that will free us to embrace the vibrant colors of each person and our world. When we see in new ways, we will see, tell, and live the story of communion.

• Fall

In the Northern Hemisphere and in the Midwest of the United States, autumn is a time of expectancy. It signals the coming arrival of the deep silence the winter darkness opens to us. Fall, with its brilliant display of color as it says goodbye, teaches us that for the new to come something must change. It offers us a way of being as we await the future.

I offer, then, a simple meditation of both listening in silence and reflecting on how the trees invite us to prepare for the next season in our lives.

Let us begin by simply becoming present to this moment. Take a few deep breaths and quiet your mind, open your heart, consent to divine mystery, God's loving presence active within you.

Pause for a few minutes.

Gaze at the trees displaying their color and the fullness of their life.

> Get in touch with how you feel as you bask in their presence and in the presence of all the trees you have enjoyed during the autumns of your life.
>
> Reflect on who or what provides a fullness in your life; who or what is coming to completion; who or what is ready to burst forth in new ways; and who or what is ready to transition.
>
> Offer thanks for the joy and gift these are and have been to you.

Listen to the leaves as they prepare for the next stage of their journey.

> **Fall, with its brilliant display of color as it says goodbye, teaches us that for the new to come something must change. It offers us a way of being as we await the future.**

The leaves are not silent as they start to get buffeted by the wind.

What feelings do you have as you deepen your awareness of change in your life, in your church, and society? How do you experience the "rustling wind"? What sounds come forth in you as you feel the shifting winds in your life: as you experience job changes; unexpected illnesses; lost relationships; and beliefs and values deeply held being questioned and challenged?

Give voice to those sounds in a prayer of lament.

What do you feel as you look at the few leaves who are holding on for dear life?

What are you holding onto for dear life? What or who, are you unable to let go of so you can prepare for what is emerging in your life?

The letting go is almost complete, as the leaves fall gently yet swiftly onto the ground.

How do you feel as you let go, or as that which you love is taken from you?

Can you feel the descent and the falling to the ground? Can you sense the next resting place for future growth?

Finally, the last leaf returns to Earth, the source of its transformation. The trees — although seemingly barren — prepare to bring forth new life in a few months.

Now is the time of expectancy ... of waiting ...

How will you wait so as to be alert to what is emerging in your life? Can you feel hope in this place of expectancy?

Pause and simply breathe again.
Stay with your experience for a few moments.
End with a simple *amen* or *namaste*, honoring the Divine within you.

• Winter

Perhaps it is the January gloom of the Great Lakes region and frigid temperatures that I have experienced that have me reflecting on how much a 'new year' looks like the old with its violence, famines, droughts, and earthquakes continuing. At such times I search for a way forward.

Then I am comforted and inspired again by Amanda Gorman in her poem "New Day's Lyric"[82]:

> Tethered by this year of yearning,
> We are learning
> That though we weren't ready for this,
> We have been readied by it.
> We steadily vow that no matter
> How we are weighed down,
> We must always pave a way forward.
>
> This hope is our door, our portal.
> Even if we never get back to normal.

No one was ready for what we have been experiencing these past years in so many areas of our life. But living through it with an awareness and a commitment to go forward has readied us for what is emerging, unfolding. We are at a threshold walking through the door, the portal, and the future is not where we came from. It will be new and we will be shaping it.

As the past disappears behind us, we become more prepared to enter the future. We find within us the energy to take the next step and propel us forward.

In her song, *A Light in the Window*, Carrie Newcomer[83] suggests an image of seeding the future in the midst of our winter.

> Off to look for a light,
> For a light
> In the window.

> *We are at a threshold walking through the door, the portal, and the future is not where we came from. It will be new and we will be shaping it.*

Now the old has already passed away,
But the new is too new to be born today.
So I'm throwing out seeds
On the winter snow
As the cold wind begins to blow,
Standing here on a new threshold.

The old has passed away. It will still take time for some things to die, to be transformed bringing forth a spring like rebirth. That newness takes time and we must play our part in its unfolding.

We can throw out seeds on the winter snow.

Standing at the threshold, readied by all that has gone before, propelled to take the next step, I find that the seeds for the birthing of the new are reflected in the fruit of the Spirit. I invite you to join me in throwing out these seeds on the winter snow ... *love, joy, peace, patience, kindness, goodness, faithfulness, gentleness, and self-control.*

Take time during these winter months, to sit in contemplative silence and allow these seeds to take root in you, nourishing you, and readying you, to take the next step. Cross the threshold, step through the portal, and become light for others to see.

• Spring

As my heart grows weary reading and listening to the news, I know I need to keep what is happening in perspective, realizing that it is part of much larger forces within the universe. Spring is a great reminder that out of death comes life, and that beauty and hope await us if we can stop and become present to it.

This brought to mind my first profession retreat led by Brother David Steindl-Rast.[84] He invited us to spend a day with each of our senses. For a certain amount of time each day, we were to focus on one of our senses and try to enter that sensation and experience it. Not analyze it, but simply be with it. It is another way of entering contemplation.

> *Spring is a great reminder that out of death comes life, and beauty and hope await us if we can stop and become present.*

Hearing
Awakening at the faintest beginnings of dawn, I lay in bed listening to the very quiet chirps of the birds outside my window. Quiet and rhythmic, the sound began to increase and seemed to be circling the house. Life was awakening, and each greeting was echoed as dawn became sunrise. Other sounds of spring: howling of the wind, staccato of raindrops on the window, river currents thrashing, clanking radiators warming the last winter chill, and ...

Seeing
Flying over the hills of Northern California, I was captivated by the stunning chartreuse of the grasses flowing for as far as my eyes could see. The beauty sank into my body, reminding me of new life and how to delight in it. Other sights of spring: watching the buds erupt overnight, acknowledging the perennials returning to grace the garden, following the baby squirrels scampering up the trees, and ...

Smelling
Catching a hint of the sweet aroma soon to fill the air as the viburnum bush in the garden beneath the window begins to

bring forth its tiny blossoms. The musky aroma of rich earth, soaked by spring rains, tickling the nostrils. Other smells of spring: tantalizing whiffs of outdoor grilling beginning to waft in the air, the sun's new warmth on my skin, the aromas embedded in wood and rocks, and …

Touching

Encountering a tree beginning to leaf, I rub the new leaves and caress the bark, feeling the texture and marveling at shape and contour. The shift in the spring wind leaves its tell-tale mark as its warmth embraces my body. Other touches of spring: clothes clinging soaked through and through from a sudden spring storm, soil sifting through fingers, stems being cut for a spring bouquet, and …

Tasting

Walking on the Santa Monica pier unencumbered by winter wear, I let my tongue savor the salty ocean air. I taste the hints of spring-sweet, refreshing, and zesty. Other tastes of spring: a hint of basil, breakfast with sweet and tart cherries, juicy peaches, tasty apricots and plums, the sweat rolling down my cheeks and into my mouth as I do my spring cleaning, and …

Taking time to be with our bodies and our senses, helps us to reconnect with ourselves and with all that is around us. Taking time reminds us that we are all connected. Taking time invites us into a stillness, a full silence, where we can let go and be present to a deeper reality of which we are a part. Taking time to welcome spring awakens us to beauty and new possibilities. Taking time prepares us to embrace the difficult times we are living in, knowing that from the seemingly bleak and dead winter, spring bursts forth. Find time to focus on each of your senses. See what you experience.

SPACIOUSNESS TO CREATE

Take time to breathe and enter the spaciousness of your heart.

For a period of time, sit in contemplation, setting the intention to be open to Divine Love within you. With your contemplative gaze, reflect on your experience in Gallery Six. Was anything evoked in you, became present to you, challenged, or shifted in you? Bring expression to it creatively through words, drawing, poetry, doodle, or ...

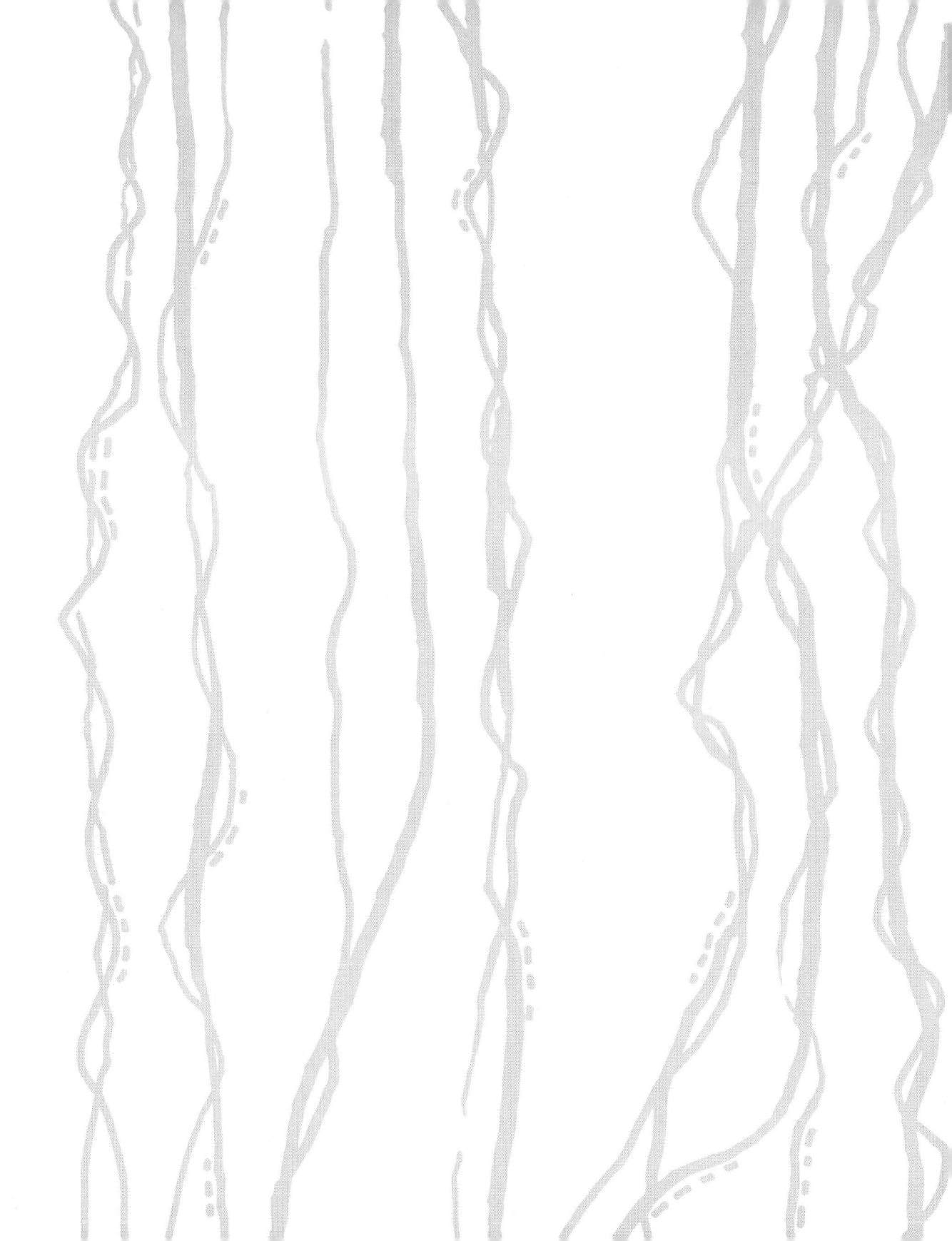

Gallery 7:

TRANSFORMING POWER OF COMMUNAL CONTEMPLATION

This is the newest room in the art gallery and is unfinished. It holds the pieces that have seeds of hope for our future—the transformative power of communal contemplation, living out the synodal[85] process in the church and world, the journey of evolutionary emergence, the role of ourselves as cosmic sentries, living out of love and forgiveness, and evolutionary hope.

- **Exercising Contemplative Power**

- **Living Synodality in a Polarized World**

- **Consider the Snail**

- **Cosmic Sentry**

- **Living Out of Love and Forgiveness**

- **Evolutionary Hope**

• Exercising Contemplative Power

'Prayer. The world's greatest wireless connection.' Those words on a sweatshirt greeted me as I opened a gift from my sister. I immediately thought this conveyed one aspect of how we understand *exercising contemplative power.*

Think about it. When we are on the Internet, we have instant access to almost anyone on this planet. Through an intricate web of electromagnetic waves, we can start a revolution — be part of a flash mob — and generate interest so that an idea or an action goes viral. Without seeing the waves radiating outward, we know we are connected.

Think about it. When we are at contemplative prayer, we set the intention to open ourselves to the Divine working within us and align our hearts and minds with this deeper reality underlying all things. Our consciousness radiates energy outward, connecting with the subtle energy fields where all minds are joined as one. There is a healing energy inherent in the Universe and we can be aligned with it. Communal contemplation is doing something. It is *contemplative power.*

Cynthia Bourgeault in her teachings on consciousness often reflects on how no conscious act is ever wasted. She understands that there is a connection between every conscious act no matter how seemingly insignificant. Each of our conscious acts connecting energetically will increase the quality and quantity of awakened consciousness on the planet.

That is not easy to grasp in our culture where the insights of Modernity continue to shape our mental operating system. Reason, measurable outcomes, and verification by our senses still trump intuition, insight, and belief in deeper dimensions of reality.

There is healing energy inherent in the Universe and we can be aligned with it.

We are learning more and more about the power of our consciousness — individual and collective — and the powerful energy field which can be created when we align our minds and hearts with the deeper reality underlying all things.

But that is changing with the advance of quantum physics. David Bohm, a leading quantum physicist of our age, developed the theory of the Implicate Order. His underlying theory posits the unbroken wholeness of the totality of existence. Within the Implicate Order, everything is connected and like a hologram, each element reveals something about the whole. Within the Implicate Order, everything is enfolded into everything. This complements the Explicate Order where things are unfolded and made manifest. Of course, I don't pretend to understand this complicated theory, but what is important is that at the deepest dimension of reality, everything is connected. There is an underlying dimension that is not accessible through our senses. This theory begins to give credence to the wisdom and insights of sages and mystics who experienced the oneness of all reality. [86]

We are learning more and more about the power of our consciousness — individual and collective — and the powerful energy field which can be created when we align our minds and hearts with the deeper reality underlying all things. Studies and experiments are increasing as more and more scientists give credence to the influence a community can have on an individual as well as the individual on the whole community through these vibratory energy fields.

This broadening interest by science is exciting. It offers another way of thinking about our world and our lives. For me, it is a real breakthrough so needed today. The insights of science interface with the wisdom of the mystics, each offering the other legitimacy as we explore who we are and why we are here.

• Living Synodality in a Polarized World

It is often said that the Catholic Church is not a democracy. Its hierarchical and monarchical governance structures have prevailed throughout the ages. However, Pope Francis is transforming the ways that those in power and authority are making decisions. The key to this is doing it together with all the people of God. The process is called synodality.[87] It is not just a skill set but rather a new way of relating to each other rooted in one's experience of the Divine.

Such a process must welcome differences and promote harmony. It acknowledges the tensions but understands that those involved can draw energy to continue moving forward. To find the hierarchy of the Church moving in this direction is very welcoming, for this synodal process is very similar to the transformative practice of contemplative dialogue.[88]

To truly encounter another who is different from you or who holds differing views is not an easy task. We see that in the growing divisions within our country and our church. We become convinced of our position or belief and consciously or unconsciously defend it, fearing change may make us look weak or unprincipled or demand more than we are willing to give.

Yet, it is only in that vulnerability and openness to the other that understanding and transformation occur.

How we foster that spirit within ourselves is for me rooted in contemplation. I believe the future that is emerging invites us to encounter deeply held assumptions, biases, beliefs, and worldviews in ways we have not known previously and for which we are not skilled.

There are few, if any, road maps for this emerging future. But I have often pondered the process by which the early church agreed to change the belief and practice that

> **Synodality is a new way of relating to each other rooted in one's experience of the Divine.**
>
> **The synodal process is very similar to the transformative practice of contemplative dialogue.**

all Gentiles be forced to convert to Judaism and to follow the law of Moses before being baptized.

In Acts 15, the evangelist wrote that the elders and apostles came together to hear advocates for the different positions. They celebrated all God had accomplished through the work of those men sent to Antioch to preach the good news to the Gentiles. They agreed to discuss this issue more thoroughly.

Peter posed a question to those assembled: "Why, then, do you put God to the test by trying to place on the shoulders of these converts a yoke which neither we nor our ancestors were able to bear?" Then the assembly fell silent.

They continued to listen to each other. James articulated what he felt was the sense of the whole: that they would not make it more difficult for Gentiles who are turning to God. The entire assembly decided to accept what James recommended.

Within this narrative, I see essential elements for us to ponder: sharing a position rooted in experience; listening to others; engaging in dialogue; asking generative questions; entering into contemplative silence; and allowing the emergence of a way forward. And, like the early church, deciding not to burden others with what we are unable to bear.

That is a synodal experience. That is a contemplative process. That is what we need in our world today.

• Consider the Snail

Consider the snail!

Recently, I encountered a snail. There was a snail, moving from a patch of grass, needing to come out of itself to cross over the pavement to the grass on the other side. Its head extended quite far out, lugging its shell behind. On its way to the other side it left a shiny trail, a sign of its presence — an acknowledgment that this snail was here and made an impression!

The snail is an earlier stage of evolutionary emergence. But we share the evolutionary journey with all those who came before and those yet to come. Each stage lives and exists in environments, in cultures, on lands appropriate for that time. Throughout our 13.8-billion-year history the containers of our unfolding have changed radically and incrementally.

We have emerged from stardust; warmed by the sun; frozen by glaciers; nourished in the oceans; walked onto land; breathed in air; lived as tribes; gathered in villages; clustered in cities; organized governments; wrote poetry; sang songs; created rituals; praised deities and ...

And like the shell on the snail's back, all of that is carried with us. Some parts of it more consciously than other parts. We have on our backs the years of how evolution unfolded. We have been shaped by it and we continue to shape it. We all have our patch of grass that feeds us; that makes us comfortable; that provides the perspective from which we view the rest of our world.

Too often we stay in that place. We believe we have all that we need. When we gaze beyond our boundaries, we either judge that we are in a better, safer place, or we are curious and wonder about what may be out there.

This day the snail began to move forward, outward. Sticking its neck out, extending way beyond its house on its

> *The snail to move forward has to stick its neck out extending way beyond its house on its back and risk going beyond its patch of grass.*
>
> *The snail was not yet on the 'other side' ... We, too, are not necessarily getting to the 'other side' or accomplishing an outcome that we've set for ourselves. Our moving forward is enough, for it, begins to create the container from which the future unfolds.*

back, it left the soft grass and experienced a rather strange sensation — concrete pavement.

As we journey in our life there are times when we stick our neck out. We are curious about the things that are not so familiar to us. We begin to move forward and outward far beyond the safety of our home. We wonder about how things are from different perspectives. We, too, experience a strange sensation when we begin to see things from the perspective of others.

Of course, the snail does this slowly. It does not move fast. It takes its time sensing everything around it as it journeys forward.

Contemplation is a form of prayer that invites us to go slowly like the snail and become aware of ourselves and of all that is around us. It invites us to enter a spaciousness that is far more than what we experience in our hectic, rational, 'me' focused life. It is within that space that we begin to move: extending our necks, risking seeing more fully what is around us, and encountering others who may be at different stages in the evolutionary process.

We often think of evolution as physical or biological. Today, many believe that the next stage of evolution is at the level of consciousness. Moving forward necessitates moving inward to enter the deep mystery of the Divine. In doing so we become free to embrace all that has gone before and what is still to come.

That evolutionary journey through the stages of consciousness is where Spiral Dynamics Integral (SDi) can help us. We begin to see an evolution of thought that parallels the way that humans have evolved related to how and where they lived, to the material conditions of their lives.[89]

All the different stages of consciousness are alive in us and among us. Like biological evolution, we are more or less aware of these different worldviews and perspectives from which we have emerged. The polarities we experience today reflect the dissonance that happens when people at different stages approach issues in a state of almost unconscious awareness. We have to — like the snail — risk sticking our neck out. We want to enter the middle space and create new conditions so that we can discuss with others what is important for our future.

The snail I encountered was not yet on the 'other side.' It was still in the middle and it left its mark from where it came.

We, too, are not necessarily getting to the 'other side' or accomplishing an outcome that we've set for ourselves. Our moving forward is enough, for it begins to create the container from which the future unfolds.

And like the snail, we will leave our footprints … whatever we do is part of the unfolding … the transformative process of contemplation invites us to the next stage of emergence, which has the potential to embrace all the earlier stages and to create new pathways forward.

• Cosmic Sentry

These days, I feel the need to be grounded ever more deeply in contemplation so I can move forward in new ways into the space that holds the tensions, contradictions, and challenges that are before us as families, as congregations, as a nation, as people of faith, as Earth community.

This is not easy. The complexity is great. There are so many levels from which 'to take a long loving look at the real.' And every time I begin to write, I realize how conflicted and contradictory I feel. All my presentations discuss the need to see the 'other' as a revelation of God; to be curious about those positions different from mine; and to see in our differences the potential for creative growth. I find myself doing this on a personal level as I try to understand the polarization that is on display among us as a nation. How our political challenges can be viewed so differently? How every issue these days seems to deepen our divisions making common ground harder and harder to find. This is the disposition of my heart as I ponder the many analyses of our current cultural and political climate and what needs and fears motivate the different sides.

Yet I also know that if I or we keep seeing everything as an extension of the hardening categories into which we place one another, how can anyone change a position? How does 'the other' get the space to come to some new realizations without needing to defend themselves all the time? Is it possible to extend trust while also staying alert to suspect behavior that may violate the values of our Constitution and the values of the Gospel?

I wish I had an answer, but what I do have is an image drawn from a couple of sources. One is the conscious circle of humanity which Cynthia Bourgeault discusses in her book, *Eye of the Heart*. The other is a story about Abba Arsenius, one of the early Desert Monks. Taking quite a bit of liberty with both of them, I find myself pondering the image of a Cosmic Sentry.[90]

> *Contemplation awakens us to a heightened reality calling us to stay awake to what is.*
>
> *A Cosmic Sentry becomes a lightning rod for the energy of divine compassion. Human yearning and divine blessing ebb and flow wordlessly across this sacred meeting ground in deep and purifying exchange.*

A Cosmic Sentry is one who offers intercessory prayer. Their entire body becomes a lightning rod for the energy of divine compassion. Human yearning and divine blessing ebb and flow wordlessly across this sacred meeting ground in deep and purifying exchange. The planet has always been held in its orbit by those solitary sentries who take on this great work. Their work casts a circle of protection around our fragile and beleaguered planet.

Another aspect to being a sentry is to signify when danger is near, as sentries never sleep! Contemplation awakens us to a heightened reality. It calls us to stay awake to what is. I imagine as communities of sentries we stand alert, ready to signal when danger is sensed both far away and immediate. We would give a wake-up call to all of us who fall asleep to the complexity of our times and the changing reality. I imagine us alerting each other to what we sense needs to be challenged or needs to be supported. Rooted in Gospel values we stand on firm ground and speak out of our moral authority. We act out of the energy of divine compassion as we write, educate, and engage in non-violent protest.

A sentry is also defined as a guard standing at a point of passage, as a gate. Perhaps we can be the gate that we open wide to freely move between worldviews and beliefs but which we may quickly close when hatred and violence try to gain the upper hand.

Somehow the image of Cosmic Sentries and the thought that we can become a community of sentries eases the discomfort in my heart. It signifies a hope beyond our own abilities and a way of staying alert to both dangers and possibilities.

Let me end with some advice that I remember from Bourgeault. She encourages us to open ourselves to whatever seems to resonate within us. We might even suspend any disbelief and allow the possibility that this kind of archetypal hope is real. We can let that sink in and realize that life isn't random but that we are cared for and carried in a much greater flow of love which will come to fullness in every one of us.

• Living Out of Love and Forgiveness

As you continue the contemplative journey you awaken to a new way of responding to what you encounter in your life. Fully awake to your own shadow you understand the complexity of each person, the daily situations you encounter, and the life conditions that surround you. The magnetic center of Divine Love holds you as you choose to respond to whatever is happening out of love without shame or blame, forgiving and not resenting those who have hurt you.

Sometimes it is hard for me to imagine responding in such a way to people and events in my life. However, I've recently been inspired by some people who responded out of love throughout their lives or in a moment of crisis.

The first is Nelson Mandela. I saw an excellent exhibit on Mandela in Detroit.[91] It chronicled Mandela's life, beginning when he was born into royalty within the Thembu Kingdom in the Transkei Territory; his years as an activist against apartheid; his time in prison having been arrested as a threat to the white South African government; his election as the first Black president of South Africa; and his years in retirement.

Walking through the exhibit, I felt great recognition. I had worked on sanctions against South Africa when I was in Washington, D.C.; I had friends who were exiled from South Africa because of their opposition to the apartheid policies; and there were IHM sisters from my congregation who served in South Africa.

I also traveled there in the 1980s and saw the effects of apartheid within the townships where the Black South Africans lived. The policies enacted by the government against Blacks — taking of their land; exploiting their labor; providing inadequate education, health care, housing, and other services; preventing them from voting; and treating

> *The magnetic center of Divine Love holds you as you choose to respond ...*
> *out of love without shame or blame, forgiving and not resenting those who have hurt you.*
>
> *Their love for their unknown neighbor trumped any fear or concern they had about themselves.*

them as inferior and less than human — were also painfully familiar in terms of the U.S. experience of slavery.

It was when I allowed Mandela's experience in prison to sink into me that I began to shift what I saw. Here was an educated man who worked tirelessly against the apartheid government. He was considered a traitor and sentenced to Robben Island, a notorious prison, for 18 years.

Here, he lived in a damp concrete cell with a straw mat. He spent his days breaking rocks into gravel being forbidden to wear sunglasses in the glaring sun, which took a toll on his eyesight.

When released from prison, he was committed to reconciliation and was willing to lead the country if elected. He was a controversial figure throughout his life. He was denounced by the right as a communist terrorist and by the left as a sellout, too eager to negotiate and reconcile with apartheid's supporters.

Nevertheless, he continued to be true to who he was as a human being. He had hope, even though he didn't know the outcome of his work, his vision of which is yet to be fulfilled in South Africa.

Amid the suffering and the injustice, he lived out of love, compassion, and forgiveness. I felt he was operating out of a different way of "seeing" reality, a different structure of consciousness that offered possibility, offered an authentic way of being human. I felt he lived from his magnetic center of Divine Love.

The second experience was my visit to Ground Zero and its museum in New York. It is sacred ground as you walk by all the names listed around the two memorial areas. I was quite aware that sacred ground exists wherever persons are annihilated by anger, terror, and revenge in such numbers, but few countries have the wherewithal to honor each by name. However, what caught my attention was a short video describing the Boatlift.[92]

As the Twin Towers collapsed, an enormous cloud of smoke and debris erupted and covered that part of Manhattan extending toward the water's edge. People were running for their lives and many headed to the water. There was no way out of that section of Manhattan by land. A call went out from the Coast Guard to anyone who had a boat nearby to come to the harbor area.

Those who were interviewed spoke about how they didn't know what they were going to encounter. They just knew they had to do it. Tugboats, tour boats, and private boats began to appear at the water's edge. The captains of those boats were hard-working folks, who even in the face of not knowing the extreme risk they would be assuming, knew they had to respond to the call.

That day, 500,000 people were transported to safety in approximately nine hours by these hundreds of vessels and their pilots who answered that call. It was the largest boatlift ever.

As I watched the video, I felt the actions of the people who responded came from the best of who we are as human beings. They did not know the outcome for themselves or for those for whom they were coming, but their love for their neighbor trumped any fear or concern they had about themselves. The Divine Love that held them, propelled them forward to respond out of love.

Finally, it is Pierre Teilhard de Chardin's life that also witnesses to living out of love and forgiveness. Teilhard (1881-1955) was an evolutionary thinker, a paleontologist, a mystic, priest, and theologian. He lived through the two world wars. He was a stretcher bearer in WWI and saw the horrors of the war.[93]

His work was controversial within the church. The Vatican forbade him to write or teach on philosophical and theological subjects and he was forbidden to publish his written works. He could not attend international conferences on paleontology and his works were not to be in libraries, sold in Catholic bookstores, or published in other languages. Eventually, his works were published posthumously by a friend to whom he had given his texts.

Teilhard wrote of hope and the power and possibility of love within the human person and humanity. Today, he is considered a major thinker, mystic, and shaper of an evolving consciousness that invites us to live out of love, compassion, forgiveness, faith, and hope. However, he died not knowing what would happen. The outcome did not drive his hope. His hope was rooted in love. He believed in the goodness of humanity and our evolutionary possibility.

As I reflected on these experiences, I saw how it is possible to respond to the events in the world and my life from that magnetic center of Divine Love. I saw how it is possible to respond out of love, compassion, and forgiveness in my life.

As I thought about these experiences, a favorite chant came to me. 'Everything before us brought us to this moment, standing on the threshold of a brand new day.' Everyone who has lived the fullness of love, witnessed a hope not rooted in outcome, and offered compassion to the world lived from the magnetic center of Divine Love which still permeates the now. They have affected who we are and the possibility of who we can be even in the midst of great suffering.

We are not alone and we are invited to continue placing these loving energies into our lives,

• Evolutionary Hope

A very good friend of mine periodically asks me: Why do you believe that we are evolving in a positive way? Why do you believe that our consciousness is developing toward greater complexity, inclusivity, and unity? As often happens, I found myself contemplating those questions.

So much is happening that points to humanity backpedaling with little movement forward. We see it in a call to return to nationalism; the acceptance of more authoritarian rulers; blaming those who are seen as different for all that is wrong; and the reassertion of U.S. unilateralism rejecting multilateralism and working in coalition with other nations to address military and economic issues.

Such a consciousness cannot be dismissed. Yet I also experience another consciousness evolving like a spiral. It emerges from those earlier understandings of who we were, takes a turn upward and outward, and begins to come around again on a wider trajectory. I see it in the greater acceptance of others as we embrace racial, religious, and gender differences; in the growing awareness that we are a planetary community as we address the reality and urgency of the climate crisis; in the deepening belief that we must work in coalition to address the military and economic violence that is tearing us apart among and within nations.

The questions shapeshift within me. Why do I believe that evolution itself has a directionality that over time expands, transcends, and includes the best of all that came before? Why do I believe that our consciousness evolves as well?

Maybe I just have to believe this to give meaning to life.

But I know there is more.

> *Love is a sacred reserve of energy; it is like the blood of spiritual evolution.*
>
> **Pierre Teilhard de Chardin wrote about harnessing for God the energies of Love and in so doing transforming the entire human community — culture, social institutions, and human consciousness.**

It is a matter of faith and hope. And love.

It is rooted in the integration of my Catholic faith and contemporary science. I consider myself to be fortunate that back in the mid-'60s I began reading Pierre Teilhard de Chardin's work.[94] He was a Jesuit priest, paleontologist, and mystic. Unlike so many who today in our postmodern world continue to see an irreconcilable difference between science and faith, Teilhard spent his life understanding the deep connections between evolution and spirituality. His insights were a challenge to my very traditional Catholic consciousness. Yet, I found a resonance and an attraction that stayed with me and developed over the years.

Teilhard believed that "It is the fire of love that is the most powerful, the most transformative, and the most spiritualizing force on earth: Love is the most universal, the most tremendous and the most mysterious of cosmic forces.... Love is the primal and universal psychic energy.... Love is a sacred reserve of energy; it is like the blood of spiritual evolution."[95]

Teilhard wrote about harnessing for God the energies of Love and in so doing transforming the entire human community — culture, social institutions, and human consciousness. Teilhard had a deep belief that a greater, stronger, more inclusive love for all people and all of life must be an integral part of the further evolution of the human species.

Teilhard explored these insights rooted in his Catholic faith. God's Word is incarnate and present not only in all humans but in all created reality; that is, God is incarnate in matter, in flesh, in all of creation, and in the cosmos.

Over the decades, I pondered Teilhard's works and later those of other theologians who developed his insights into an ecological spirituality bringing a new awareness to the beauty of each person and all creation. I began to understand my Christian faith in a new way that integrated the science and cosmology of our time. I understood how each of us is responsible for living the Gospel of love concretely in our lives. We move forward with a greater sense of the whole — a belief in communion, a unity that embraces diversity.

This process takes place slowly in evolutionary time.

Teilhard's insights are rooted in Jesus' love for all people regardless of faith, gender, economic class, or cultural bias. Bringing that to contemplation deepened my own belief in this amazing evolutionary process of which we are a part.

I have to have faith and hope in who we are becoming. Change is happening. As with evolution, there are times of great creativity and destruction. We have only our one life to offer to shape how the future emerges. We have a responsibility to let God be God within us. That is what contemplation invites us to — to be open to God working within us.

If we can do this, then perhaps over time, the energies of love will be harnessed and Teilhard's prayer will be fulfilled:

> *Someday, after mastering the winds, the waves, the tides and gravity, we shall harness for God the energies of love, and then, for the second time in the history of the world, humanity will have discovered fire.*[96]

SPACIOUSNESS TO CREATE

Take time to breathe and enter the spaciousness of your heart.

For a period of time, sit in contemplation, setting the intention to be open to Divine Love within you. With your contemplative gaze, reflect on your experience in Gallery Seven. Was anything evoked in you, became present to you, challenged, or shifted in you? Bring expression to it creatively through words, drawing, poetry, doodle, or …

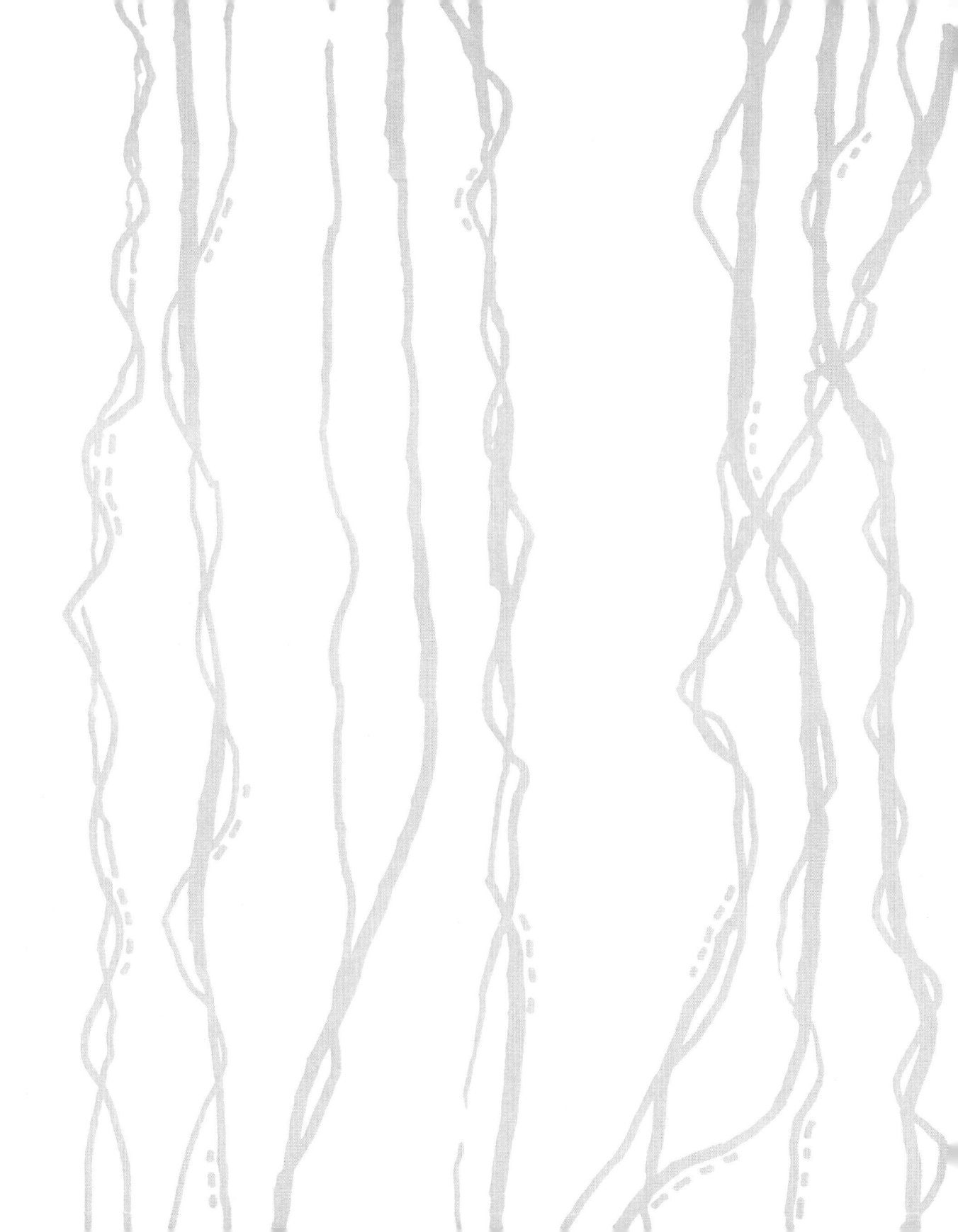

Notes

[1] Constance FitzGerald, OCD, "The Desire for God and the Transformative Power of Contemplation," in *Light Burdens, Heavy Blessings,* ed. Mary Heather MacKinnon, Moni McIntyre, and Mary Ellen Sheehan (Quincy, IL: Franciscan Press, 2000), 203.

[2] Christopher Fry, *A Sleep of Prisoners* (poem), accessed June 22, 2024, https://someinspiration.com/sleep-of-prisoners/

[3] The pieces in Galleries Three through Seven are curated from the many reflections I've written for Global Sisters Report, a project of *National Catholic Reporter*, from 2014-2024. Although a specific historical event may have inspired the piece, the message continues to be relevant.

[4] Pope Francis distinguishes between a "journey faith" and a "laboratory-faith" in the Jesuit magazine, *America,* September 30, 2013. "There is always the lurking danger of living in a laboratory. Ours is not a lab faith, 'but a journey faith,' a historical faith. God has revealed himself as history, not as a compendium of abstract truths."

[5] Sr. Wendy Beckett and Robert Ellsberg, *Dearest Sister Wendy: A Surprising Story of Faith and Friendship* (Maryknoll, NY: Orbis Books, 2022), 38. Ellsberg writes: "I am very moved by Pope Francis's words about a 'journey faith' a faith that emerges and unfolds on a journey, which may have twists and turns, stumbling and uncertainty rather than a 'lab faith' in which everything is clear cut and neatly defined."

[6] Illia Delio, *The Not-Yet-God: Carl Jung, Teilhard de Chardin, and the Relational Whole* (Maryknoll, NY: Orbis Books, 2023), 141.

[7] Delio, *The Not-Yet-God*, 150.

[8] Pierre Teilhard de Chardin, SJ, (1881-1955) was a Jesuit priest, an evolutionary thinker, a paleontologist, mystic, and theologian. His experience of the Divine was intimately connected with his experience of the world. He developed a holistic spirituality of mind, body, and matter grounded in an evolutionary dynamic.
Thomas Merton, OCSO, (1915-1968) was a Trappist monk, theologian, poet, spiritual writer, and social activist. He was a proponent of interfaith understanding and explored Eastern religions through his study of mystic practice pioneering dialogue with many Asian spiritual leaders.

[9] 1971 Synod of Bishops, "Justice in the World." Justicia-in-Mundo.pdf (cctwincities.org)

[10] For more information, see Mara D. Rutten, *Called to Action: NETWORK's 50 Years of Political Ministry*. (Mara D Rutten, 2023). www.networklobby.org

[11] You will find that throughout the book I have tried to offer a variety of ways to refer to God. I wanted to evoke possibilities beyond the more traditional image of a very human person who is too often seen as male as well as embodying other attributes considered normative in society.

[12] Over the years, I have drawn extensively on the work of both Thomas Keating, OCSO, and Cynthia Bourgeault which is reflected in my own prayer and writings. Cynthia Bourgeault is a modern day mystic, Episcopal priest, writer, and internationally respected speaker and retreat leader. Thomas Keating, OCSO, a Trappist monk and priest helped co-found Contemplative Outreach, Ltd., an international and ecumenical spiritual network that teaches Centering Prayer. I have interpreted their work and take full responsibility for my understanding of their thinking. I encourage you to read their original texts, many of which are listed in the bibliography. In addition to the books in the bibliography their websites are a rich resource in exploring their work in more detail. For Centering Prayer: https://www.contemplativeoutreach.org   For Cynthia Bourgeault: https://www.cynthiabourgeault.org

[13] Constance FitzGerald, OCD, is a member of the Carmelite Community in Baltimore, Maryland and a theologian. She has been a leader in her own community and in the formation of the various associations of Contemplative Sisters in the United States. Her research and writings focus on the great Carmelite mystics with a special emphasis on St. John of the Cross. Her article, *Impasse and Dark Night*, inspired both my LCWR Presidential address and the founding of the Institute for Communal Contemplation and Dialogue (ICCD). Connie became a key consultant to ICCD in its formation although I have interpreted her work and take full responsibility for my understanding of her thinking. Many of her writings focus on the transformative power of contemplation. Seven of her original works together with ten additional essays by theologians responding to her work can be found in Laurie Cassidy and M. Shawn Copeland, eds. *Desire, Darkness, and Hope* (Collegeville, MN: Liturgical Press Academic, 2021).

[14] The Leadership Conference of Women Religious (LCWR) represents the elected leadership of the majority of the congregations of women religious in the United States. While in the Presidency — a three-person triumvirate of past president, president, and vice-president — we traveled yearly to the Vatican in Rome to meet with the various dicasteries that relate to the work of women religious. Dicasteries are the departments of the Roman Curia. The most important one for women religious is the Dicastery for Institutes of Consecrated Life and Societies of Apostolic Life.

[15] The Presidential Address: *Risk the Sacred Journey* can be found at https://iccdinstitute.org/lcwr-address/ Risk the Sacred Journey, Presidential Address.

[16] Constance FitzGerald, OCD, "Impasse and Dark Night," in *Desire, Darkness, and Hope: Theology in a Time of Impasse*, eds. Laurie Cassidy and M. Shawn Copeland (Collegeville, MN: Liturgical Press, 2021), 77-102.
Impasse is more than mere conflict. FitzGerald described both the signs and the significance of impasse. These include: a breakdown of communication; the inability to right a situation despite good and well-intentioned efforts; the dwindling of hope; the rise of disillusionment; and an obsession with the problem. She discusses the spiritual significance of these "no way out" experiences and how the Holy Spirit educates and transforms us through what she calls these inescapable and uninvited impasse experiences. Within this interpretative framework, what looks and feels like disintegration and meaninglessness is, at a more profound but hidden level of faith, a process of purification leading to a resurrection experience. To embrace the impasse or dark night is to free the Spirit to push us in the direction of intuition, imagination, contemplative reflection, and ongoing discernment. *Constance FitzGerald, "Impasse and Dark Night"* can also be found at https://iccdinstitute.org /impasse-and-dark-night/

[17] The first program the Institute offered was Engaging Impasse: Circles of Contemplation and Dialogue. Those who participated in these circles were leaders who had worked to effect significant change within ecclesial and societal arenas. Rooted in their faith, they had a growing awareness of the interconnection and complexity of the issues. They realized that new responses had to go to the root of the unjust structures and that the call was for the transformation of culture and consciousness.
These leaders experienced situations of impasse, of powerlessness, as they continued their work of transformation. They realized that all the ways they knew for achieving dialogue, effecting change and influencing others were not enough. They believed that our current constructs of thought are incapable of addressing these colliding forces in a way necessary for the survival of our planet. They believed that we must engage all our ways of knowing including one open to the power of God.
The contemplative experience offers another way of entering the breakdown of societal structures and dominant worldviews. In FitzGerald's view it invites us to enter the pain and powerlessness of the impasse as an experience of societal, ecclesial, or planetary dark night as understood by the Spanish mystic, John of the Cross. Believing that God is profoundly present in the darkness and futility of the impasse, we can open ourselves to the divine energy that yields the possibility of new imagination and a new way of being and acting.
To read about the process of the program as well as participant essays reflecting their new awareness of how to engage impasse go to https://iccdinstitute.org/product/crucible-for-change/ for the book, Nancy Sylvester,

IHM and Mary Jo Klick, *Crucible for Change, Engaging Impasse through Communal Contemplation and Dialogue* (San Antonio, TX: Sor Juana Press, 2004).

[18] Because I am often asked about the authors I've studied and read I have included an extensive bibliography listing many of the resources which I have used on my *Journey-Faith*.

[19] Charles Darwin (1809-1882) was an English naturalist, geologist, and biologist. His most known contributions are in evolutionary biology. He postulated that all species of life have descended from a common ancestor. Thomas Berry, CP, (1914-2009), a Passionist priest, was a scholar of world religions and Earth history. He called himself a 'geologian' for his commitment to responding to the ecological and climate crises. He proposed and wrote about the need for a 'New Story' of evolution to inspire and guide our functioning as individuals and as a species. Brian Swimme is an evolutionary cosmologist whose primary field of research is the nature of the evolutionary dynamics of the universe. Swimme's concern is also with the role of the human within the whole Earth community, the cultural implications of evolution, and the role of humanity in the unfolding story of Earth and cosmos. Swimme and Berry were friends and collaborators for many years.

[20] Ken Wilber is an American philosopher and writer on Transpersonal Psychology and his own Integral Theory, a systematic philosophy that suggests the continuing creative integration of all human knowledge and experience. He developed the integral approach to addressing the issues of today using his AQAL framework of evolving quadrants, levels, lines, states, and types in service of individual, social, and cultural human development. Don Beck (1937-2022) was a teacher, geopolitical advisor, and theorist focusing on applications of large-scale psychology, including social psychology, evolutionary psychology, and organizational psychology, and their effect on human sociocultural systems. Together with Christopher Cowen, he is the co-author of *Spiral Dynamics: Mastering Values, Leadership, and Change*, an evolutionary human development model adapted from the work of his mentor and colleague, developmental psychologist Clare W. Graves (1914-1986). Dr. Beck has applied *Spiral Dynamics: Mastering Values, Leadership, and Change* to real-life situations and global conflicts in South Africa, the Middle East, Europe, and other areas of the world.

[21] Spiral Dynamics Integral (SDi) is an evolutionary biological, psychosocial, and spiritual developmental process that clarifies individual and collective stages, value systems, and life conditions in order to resolve conflicts and create new, emerging possibilities for peace and well-being in a changing complex world. It is based on the original work of developmental psychologist Clare W. Graves who began a longitudinal research activity designed to try to figure out why people think in different ways about virtually everything from politics to religion to sports to architecture to economic theories to sex and marriage to a host of other kinds of issues. What he discovered was that all the various schools of psychology, the different theories, rather than being contradictory of each other are simply different stages of psychological development. Eventually he was able to describe this finding in what now is called Spiral Dynamics. The basic concept is based on an upward moving spiral, indicating that as a spiral unfolds, it moves to greater complexity. Each of the turns of the spiral represents a different worldview, a weltanschauung, a way of understanding reality. At each turn, or stage, there are new beliefs, values and behaviors as each stage is transcended while including the wisdom of previous stages. See Don Edward Beck and Christopher Cowan, *Spiral Dynamics: Mastering Values, Leadership, and Change*.
Also see: https://iccdinstitute.org/integration-2/
https://iccdinstitute.org/what-is-spiral-dynamics-integral/

[22] Paul Levy, *The Quantum Revelation: A Radical Synthesis of Science and Spirituality*. (New York: Select Books, 2018), xxix. In his introduction to *The Quantum Revelation*, Levy writes:
"Quantum theory is teaching us that implicit in our very thinking are certain flaws and misperceptions that, unseen and taken for granted, unnecessarily constrain and limit our ability to apprehend the nature of nature, including our own. The founders of quantum physics — often times referred to as 'genius physicists' — people such as Max Planck, Albert Einstein, Niels Bohr, Werner Heisenberg, Wolfgang Pauli, and Erwin Schrödinger, famously argued that quantum physics is first and foremost a new way of thinking. Indeed, the most far-reaching impact 'of that uniquely twentieth century mode of thought, quantum physics,' will be found within the human mind."

Levy continues, "The discoveries of quantum physics require a novel response in us which, when more fully understood and integrated, will irrevocably change us — both individually and as a species — in the very core of our being. Regarding the implications of quantum physics, John Bell, one of the most important physicists of the latter half of the twentieth century, is of the opinion that the new way of seeing things will involve an imaginative leap that will astonish us. It is hard to imagine something truly astonishing that we wouldn't tend to initially rule out as preposterous. This new way of seeing things, this imaginative leap, is truly an evolutionary up-leveling, a real quantum jump in consciousness, in which quantum physics is inviting each of us to partake."

[23] ICCD's program, *Enter the Chaos: Engage the Differences to Make a Difference*, integrates evolution, development of consciousness, and contemplation to explore why there are such polarities today and the potential for transformation. https://iccdinstitute.org/enter-the-chaos/
www.iccdinstitute.org

[24] Karl Rahner, "Christian Living Formerly and Today," in *Theological Investigations VII*, trans. David Bourke (New York: Herder and Herder, 1971),15 as quoted in Harvey D. Egan, *Soundings in the Christian Mystical Tradition* (Collegeville, MN: Liturgical Press, 2010), 338.

[25] For over twenty plus years my understanding of contemplation has been shaped by many sources. Constance FitzGerald, OCD, Cynthia Bourgeault, and Thomas Keating, OCSO, have been most significant, having read many of their works and attended multiple programs explaining their perspectives. I have drawn on their insights in talks, processes, and articles I've written for varied audiences, including this Gallery section. I have interpreted their work and take full responsibility for my understanding of their thinking. I encourage you to read their original texts, many of which are listed in the bibliography.

[26] Beatrice Bruteau, *The Holy Thursday Revolution* (Maryknoll, NY: Orbis Books, 2005), 5-7.
Much is written about consciousness today but I find the work of Beatrice Bruteau, especially in *The Holy Thursday Revolution,* extremely helpful in reflecting on how the development of consciousness intersects with one's deeper transformation. Considering Jesus' exhortation 'Love your neighbor as yourself,' Bruteau understands that one cannot love one's neighbor as oneself because we do not perceive the neighbor as our self, but rather as a threat. Bruteau believes to change our perceptions we must get in touch with the worldview we are operating out of and its assumptions. "When these assumptions are brought up to consciousness and seen to be assumptions about the structure of reality, it then becomes possible to think about substituting an alternative set of assumptions, that is, another worldview. The shift from one view to the other is the revolution." This capacity to create the spaciousness to perceive in new ways reflects the transformative power of contemplation. Beatrice Bruteau (1930-2014) was a pioneer in interspirituality and contemplative thinking. She was a contemplative, scholar, teacher, and explorer of evolutionary consciousness.

[27] See endnotes #21 and #26.

[28] Non-discursive prayer is known as apophatic prayer and praying with words is called cataphatic. For a more complete understanding of contemplation and the classical mystical journey read Constance FitzGerald, OCD's works in *Desire, Darkness and Hope* as well as Teresa of Avila, *Interior Castle* and St. John of the Cross, *Dark Night of the Soul*.

[29] Cynthia Bourgeault, *The Heart of Centering Prayer: Nondual Christianity in Theory and Practice*. (Boulder, CO: Shambhala Publications, 2016), 33.

[30] Thomas Merton also understood the importance of being in touch with one's authentic self before trying to help others. "One who attempts to act for others or for the world without deepening one's own self-understanding, freedom, integrity, and capacity to love, will have nothing to give others. One will communicate to them nothing but the contagion of one's own obsessions, aggressiveness, ego-centered ambitions, delusions about ends and means, doctrinaire prejudices, and ideas."

Lawrence S. Cunningham, ed. *Thomas Merton: Spiritual Master, The Essential Writings*. https://www.goodreads.com/quotes/8358369-he-who-attempts-to-act-and-do-things-for-others

[31] The basis for this teaching is Thomas Keating's psychology of Centering Prayer which he called the Divine Therapy. See Thomas Keating, *The Human Condition: Contemplation and Transformation* (Mahway, NJ: Paulist Press, 1999).; Cynthia Bourgeault, *Centering Prayer and Inner Awakening* (New York: Cowley, 2004), 91-99.; Bourgeault, *The Heart of Centering Prayer*, 29-39.; *Welcoming Prayer Consent on the Go*, Contemplative Outreach, 2014, 9-14.

[32] Engaging in Deepening Conversation, Institute for Communal Contemplation and Dialogue https://iccdinstitute.org/engaging-in-deepening-conversation/

[33] https://iccdinstitute.org/dialogue-and-moms-hash. Gratitude for Jean Alvarez's permission to reprint her article here.

[34] See Gallery Two: Witnessing Presence.

[35] In Spiral Dynamics Integral (SDi), the work of bringing all the perspectives from the various stages of consciousness together and to imagine a future that addresses the greatest good for everyone is called meshweaving.

[36] See endnote #21.

[37] Thank you to Alan Krema from Contemplative Outreach Chicago who suggested this practice. www.centeringprayerchicago.org.

[38] Constance FitzGerald, OCD, "The Transformation in Wisdom, the Subversive Character and Educative Power of Sophia and Contemplation," in *Desire, Darkness, and Hope: Theology in a Time of Impasse*, eds. Laurie Cassidy and M. Shawn Copeland (Collegeville, MN: Liturgical Press, 2021), 303-304.

[39] FitzGerald, "The Transformation in Wisdom, the Subversive Character and Educative Power of Sophia and Contemplation," 269.

[40] FitzGerald, "The Transformation in Wisdom, the Subversive Character and Educative Power of Sophia and Contemplation," 304.

[41] Believing language is critical to shaping how we think, I've chosen to use the word 'kindom' instead of kingdom to signify that Jesus was not advocating a political structure but more of a familial one where we are all kin.

[42] Pope Francis, *Laudato Si', On Care for Our Common Home* (Vatican City: Libreria Editrice Vaticana, 2015), #159.

[43] DACA stands for Deferred Action for Childhood Arrivals, a US immigration policy that allows some individuals with unlawful presence in the United States, after being brought to the country as children, to receive a renewable two-year period of deferred action from deportation and become eligible for an employment work permit. The Dream Act would permanently protect certain immigrants who came to the United States as children but who are vulnerable to deportation. The first version of the Dream Act [Development, Relief, and Education for Alien Minors] was introduced in 2001.

[44] The pandemic refers to the global health emergency known as Covid-19 initially discovered in Wuhan, China in 2019. In the United States, the Centers for Disease Control and Prevention (CDC) alerted Americans of the outbreak abroad in January 2020. By March 2020, the World Health Organization (WHO) declared a global health emergency. On January 30, 2023, the Biden Administration announced it would end the Covid-19 public health emergency declarations on May 11, 2023.

[45] George Floyd was a black American man who was murdered by a white police officer in Minneapolis, MN during an arrest made over the suspected use of a counterfeit twenty-dollar bill on May 25, 2020.

[46] ©Nan C. Merrill, 2003, *Psalms for Praying: An Invitation to Wholeness*, Continuum US, an imprint of Bloomsbury Publishing Plc., 30.

[47] Begun in 1990 as a coalition from 16 Catholic faith communities, Future Church seeks changes that will provide all Roman Catholics the opportunity to participate fully in Church life, ministry, and governance. FutureChurch – https://futurechurch.org

[48] Merrill, *Psalms for Praying*, 29.

[49] Mary Mrozowski developed the Welcoming Prayer, or Welcoming Practice, as it is also known, in the late 1980s. It is a simple but extraordinary powerful prayer flowing from Centering Prayer, which invites us to let go and surrender into God dwelling within us. First, focus, feel, and sink into what you are experiencing in your body at this moment. Get in touch with the sensation, be it a physical pain or an emotion. You do not analyze it. You simply feel it. Second, welcome, embrace what is happening within you. You say, "Welcome, pain," "Welcome, anger," or whatever the feeling is. This counterintuitive teaching works. By focusing on the feeling and embracing it, you actually release its hold on you, removing its power to hurt you. One important distinction: You are only welcoming the physical or psychological content of the moment; you are not welcoming an external situation. For example, you wouldn't say, "Welcome, cancer," but rather, you would welcome what you are feeling because you have cancer, so you might say, "Welcome, fear." Third, Let Go. Saying the next two sentences consent to being transformed by dismantling our emotional programs for the healing of our unconscious. They are: "I let go of the desire for security, affection, control" and "I let go of the desire to change what I am experiencing." For more information: Pamela Begeman, Mary Dwyer, Cherry Haisten, Gail Fitzpatrick-Hopler, and Therese Saulnier, *Welcoming Prayer Consent on the Go* (Wilkes-Barre, PA: Contemplative Outreach, 2014).

[50] Merrill, *Psalms for Praying*, 27.

[51] Merrill, *Psalms for Praying*, 25.

[52] Pema Chodron (1936-) is an American Tibetan-Buddhist ordained nun. She has written several books and had been the principal teacher at Gampo Abbey in Nova Scotia until she retired in 2020. One of Pema Chodron's best known teachings is that of Tonglen, a counter intuitive approach to suffering and pain.
   The practice invites you to begin by breathing in the suffering and breathing out a gift. Then focus on a person or a group of people who are suffering. Feel their suffering and breathe it in. Concentrate on the 'in' breath of suffering for about 3-5 minutes. Do not worry about the 'out' breath at this time. Then choose a gift to breathe out to that person or group who are suffering. Try to feel it-to make it very tangible. Concentrate on the 'out' breath of gift for about 3-5 minutes. Don't worry about the 'in' breath. Then put the 'in' breath and the 'out' breath together for another 3-5 minutes. Notes by Jean Alvarez from *Engaging Impasse: Circles of Contemplation and Dialogue*. More information https://tricycle.org/beginners/buddhism/tonglen/

[53] The Sandy Hook Elementary School shooting was a mass shooting that occurred on December 14, 2012 in Newtown, Connecticut.

[54] Colin Woodard, *American Nations: A History of the Eleven Rival Regional Cultures of North America* (New York: Penguin Books, 2022).

[55] Jill Long Thompson, "The Character of American Democracy: Values-Based Leadership," Brookings Institution, (November 12, 2020).
https://www.brookings.edu/articles/the-character-of-american-democracy-values-based-leadership/

[56] See endnote #21.

[57] For more about this shift in worldviews see https://iccdinstitute.org/shifting-worldviews/

[58] See endnote #22.

[59] Thomas Merton, *Seven Story Mountain* (New York: Harcourt, 1948).

[60] Constance FitzGerald, OCD, "From Impasse to Prophetic Hope: Crisis of Memory," in *Desire, Darkness, and Hope: Theology in a Time of Impasse*, eds. Laurie Cassidy and M. Shawn Copeland (Collegeville, MN: Liturgical Press, 2021), 447-448. Or https://iccdinstitute.org/from-impasse-to-prophetic-hope-crisis-of-memory/

[61] Merrill, *Praying the Psalms*, 293-294.

[62] Thomas B. Edsall, "When It Comes to Eating Away at Democracy, Trump is a Winner," New York Times, August 24, 2022. https://www.nytimes.com/2022/08/24/opinion/us-trump.html

[63] Brother David Steindl-Rast, OSB, is an Austrian-American Catholic Benedictine monk, author, and lecturer. He is committed to interfaith dialogue and has dealt with the interaction between spirituality and science. Brother David was a good friend of my religious community and was instrumental in the national House of Prayer Movement during the late 1960's and early 1970's. IHM Sisters Ann Chester, IHM, and Margaret Brennan, IHM, were leaders in this effort. He was invited to give the retreat in 1969 to those of us who were completing the novitiate and taking our first vows.

[64] FitzGerald, "Impasse and Dark Night,"102.

[65] Pope Francis, *The Joy of the Gospel, Evangelii Gaudium* (Washington, DC: USCCB,2013), #183.

[66] See endnote #8.

[67] Teilhard de Chardin, *A Book of Hours*, eds. Kathleen Deignan, CND and Libby Osgood, CND (Maryknoll, NY: Orbis Books, 2023). The original work of Teilhard from which the quote is taken is in parenthesis after the quote. The pages in *A Book of Hours* are as follows: 5(DM 46-47); 37 (HU 114-115); 220 (TF 119-120).

[68] Corita Kent (1918-1986) was a sister of the Immaculate Heart of Mary congregation of Los Angeles, CA. She was an artist whose primary medium was serigraphy or screen painting. Her artwork often contained messages of love and peace which were quite popular during the social movements of the 1960's and 1970's.

[69] See endnote #8.

[70] Rupert Sheldrake, Terence McKenna, and Ralph Abraham, *Chaos, Creativity, and Cosmic Consciousness* (Rochester, Vermont: Park Street Press, 2001), 174.
  Rupert Sheldrake is the former director of studies in biochemistry and cell biology at Cambridge University. He has developed a vision of a living, developing universe with its own inherent memory. His hypothesis includes the concepts of Formative Causation, Morphic Resonance and Morphogenetic Field. Morphic fields play a causal role in morphogenesis (the coming into being of form). These fields contain an inherent memory, transmitted from previous similar systems by morphic resonance and tend to become increasingly habitual. These fields include behavioral, social, cultural, mental, and morphogenetic fields. Morphogenetic fields as posited by Sheldrake also contain an inherent memory transmitted from similar past organisms by the process of morphic resonance. Morphic resonance involves the transmission of formative influences through or across time and space without a decrease due to distance or lapse of time.

[71] John Scottus Eriugena, who signed himself as "Eriugena," was a teacher, theologian, philosopher, and poet. He is considered the most significant Irish intellectual in the early monastic period.

[72] John Philip Newell, *Sacred Earth, Sacred Soul: Celtic Wisdom for Reawakening to What Our Souls Know and Healing the World* (New York, NY: HarperCollins, 2021).

[73] Jan Richardson, *Circle of Grace: A Book of Blessings for the Seasons* (Orlando, FL: Wanton Gospeller Press), 67. © Jan Richardson. Janrichardson.com

[74] I am drawing on the insights of Cynthia Bourgeault for this section, primarily her work:
Cynthia Bourgeault, *The Holy Trinity and the Law of Three: Discovering the Radical Truth at the Heart of Christianity* (Boston, MA: Shambhala Publication, 2013), 73.

[75] Bourgeault, *The Holy Trinity and the Law of Three*, 74.

[76] Cynthia Bourgeault, *Wisdom Jesus: Transforming Heart and Mind – A New Perspective on Christ and His Message* (Boston, MA: Shambhala Publications, 2008), 73.

[77] Thomas Keating, *Reflections on the Unknowable* (Brooklyn, NY: Lantern Books, 2014), 33.

[78] Bruteau, *Holy Thursday Revolution*, 55-60.

[79] Cynthia Bourgeault, *Eye of the Heart: A Spiritual Journey into the Imaginal Realm* (Boulder, CO: Shambhala, 2020). Because I'm drawing on insights of Cynthia's and summarizing a very complicated subject in a small space, I recommend that you read her book *Eye of the Heart*, as well as *The Wisdom Jesus*.

[80] Bourgeault, *Wisdom Jesus*, 134.

[81] Bourgeault, *Wisdom Jesus*, 133-134.

[82] Poetry.com, STANDFS4LLC, 2024 "New Day's Lyric" Accessed May 28, 2024. https://www.poetry.com/poem/11834/new day's-lyric.

[83] Carrie Newcomer. "A Light in the Window." Track 4 on *A Permeable Life*. 2014. A+Permeable+Life+(+Website+Lyrics)+.pdf (squarespace.com)

[84] See endnote #63.

[85] "Synodality means journeying together as the People of God. It indicates a way of listening to each individual person as a member of the Church to understand how God might be speaking to all of us." Laudato Si' Movement. www.laudatosimovement.org

[86] David Bohm, *Wholeness and the Implicate Order* (New York: Routledge, 1980).

[87] See endnote #85.

[88] See Gallery Two: Contemplative Dialogue.

[89] See endnote #21.

[90] Cynthia Bourgeault, *Eye of the Heart*, 139-156.
  https://orthodoxwiki.org/Sayings_of_the_Desert_Fathers

[91] mandela-the-official-exhibition.

[92] boatlift-tom-hanks-narrates-untold-tale-911-resilience.

[93] See endnote #8.

[94] See endnote #8.

[95] Ursula King, *Christ in All Things: Exploring Spirituality with Pierre Teilhard de Chardin* (Maryknoll, NY: Orbis Books, 2016), 78.

[96] Pierre Teilhard de Chardin, *Toward the Future*, trans. René Hague (New York: Harcourt, 1973), 86-87.

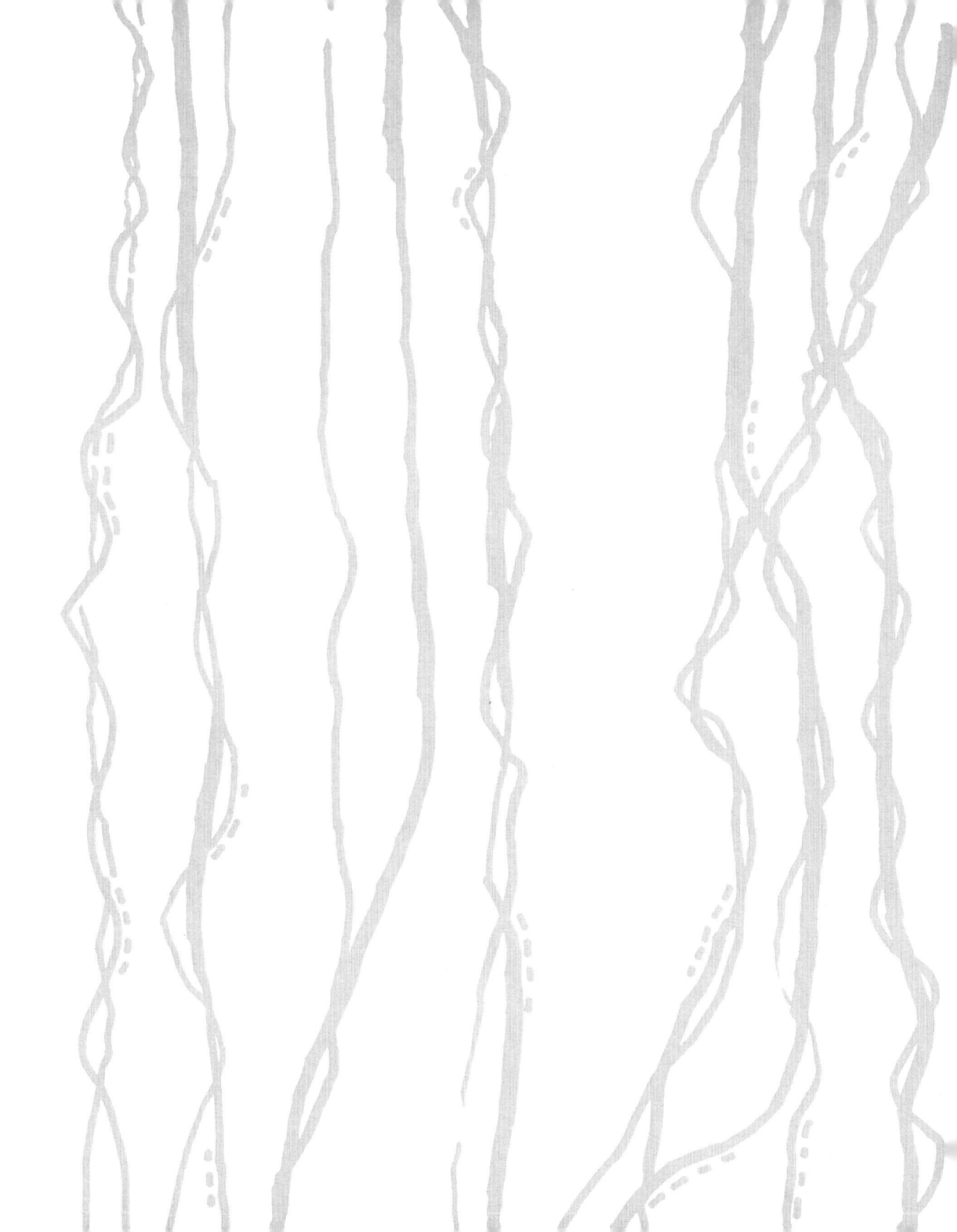

Bibliography

Abram, David. *The Spell of the Sensuous*. New York: Vintage Books, 1996.

Allen, Marcia, CSJ, and Gilla Dube, CSJ. eds. *With Fire and Passion, the Mysticism of Bette Moslander, CSJ*. Salina, KS: Consolidated Publishing, 2020.

Almaas, A. H. *Facets of Unity: The Enneagram of Holy Ideas*. Berkeley, CA: Diamond Books, 1998.

Arbuckle, Gerald A. *Refounding the Church*. Maryknoll, NY: Orbis Books, 1993.

Bauman, Lynn. *The Gospel of Thomas, Wisdom of the Twin*. Ashland, OR: White Cloud Press, 2012.

Beck, Don. *Spiral Dynamics Integral*. Video Series. Sounds True.

Beck, Don Edward and Christopher Cowan. *Spiral Dynamics: Mastering Values, Leadership, and Change*. Malden, MA: Blackwell Publishing, 2005.

Bellah, Robert, Richard Madsen, William Sullivan, Ann Swidler, and Steven Tipton. *Habits of the Heart: Individualism and Commitment in American Life.* Berkeley, CA: University of California Press, 1985.

Berry, Thomas. *The Dream of the Earth*. San Francisco: Sierra Club Books, 1988.

Berry, Thomas. *The Great Work: Our Way into the Future.* New York: Bell Tower, 1999.

Berry, Thomas. *Evening Thoughts: Reflecting on Earth as a Sacred Community.* Edited by Mary Evelyn Tucker. San Francisco: Sierra Club Books, 2006.

Berry, Thomas. *Selected Writings on the Earth Community*. Maryknoll, NY: Orbis Books, 2014.

Berry, Thomas and Thomas Clarke. *Befriending the Earth: A Theology of Reconciliation Between Humans and the Earth*. Mystic, CT: Twenty-third Publications, 1995.

Boff, Leonardo. *Ecology and Liberation: A New Paradigm*. Maryknoll, NY: Orbis, 1995.

Bohm, David. *Wholeness and the Implicate Order.* New York: Routledge, 1980.

Bohm, David. *On Dialogue*. London: Routledge, 1996.

Borg, Marcus J. *Meeting Jesus Again for the First Time: The Historical Jesus and the Heart of Contemporary Faith*. San Francisco: Harper San Francisco, 1994.

Bourgeault, Cynthia. *Mystical Hope: Trusting in the Mercy of God*. Lanham, MD: Cowley Publications, 2001.

Bourgeault, Cynthia. *The Wisdom Way of Knowing: Reclaiming an Ancient Tradition to Awaken the Heart*. San Francisco: Jossey-Bass, 2003.

Bourgeault, Cynthia. *The Wisdom Jesus: Transforming Heart and Mind – A New Perspective on Christ and His Message*. Boston, MA: Shambhala, 2008.

Bourgeault, Cynthia. *The Meaning of Mary Magdalene: Discovering the Woman at the Heart of Christianity*. Boston, MA: Shambhala, 2010.

Bourgeault, Cynthia. *The Holy Trinity and the Law of Three: Discovering the Radical Truth at the Heart of Christianity*. Boston, MA: Shambhala, 2013.

Bourgeault, Cynthia. *The Heart of Centering Prayer: Nondual Christianity in Theory and Practice*. Boulder, CO: Shambhala Press, 2016.

Bourgeault, Cynthia. *Eye of the Heart: A Spiritual Journey into the Imaginal Realm*. Boulder, CO: Shambhala Publications, 2020.

Bourgeault, Cynthia. *The Corner of Fourth and Nondual. My Theology.* Minneapolis, MN: Fortress Press, 2022.

Brown, Michael. *The Presence Process*. Vancouver, Canada: Namaste Publishing, 2010.

Brink, Laurie. *The Heavens Are Telling the Glory of God*. Collegeville, MN: Liturgical Press, 2022.

Brady, Mark, ed. *The Wisdom of Listening*. Boston, MA: Wisdom Publications, 2003.

Brown, Raymond E. *The Churches the Apostles Left Behind*. Mahwah, NJ: Paulist Press, 1984.

Brueggemann, Walter. *Hopeful Imagination: Prophetic Voices in Exile*. Philadelphia, PA: Fortress Press, 1986.

Brueggemann, Walter. *Hope Within History*. Atlanta, GA: John Knox Press, 1987.

Brueggemann, Walter. *Tenacious Solidarity: Biblical Provocations on Race, Religion, Climate, and the Economy*. Minneapolis, MN: Fortress Press, 2010.

Brueggemann, Walter. *The Practice of Prophetic Imagination*. Minneapolis, MN: Fortress Press, 2012.

Brueggemann, Walter. *Real World Faith*. Minneapolis, MN: Fortress Press, 2023.

Bruteau, Beatrice. *Radical Optimism, Rooting Ourselves in Reality*. New York: Crossroad, 1993.

Bruteau, Beatrice. *God's Ecstasy: The Creation of a Self-Creating World*. New York: Crossroad, 1997.

Bruteau, Beatrice. *The Grand Option: Personal Transformation and a New Creation*. Notre Dame, IN: University of Notre Dame Press, 2001.

Bruteau, Beatrice. *The Holy Thursday Revolution*. Maryknoll, NY: Orbis Books, 2005.

Bryson, Bill. *A Short History of Nearly Everything*. London: Doubleday, 2003.

Callahan, William R. *Noisy Contemplation*. Brentwood, MD: Quixote Center, 2008.

Campbell, Camille. *Meditations with Teresa of Avila*. Santa Fe, NM: Bear & Company, 1985.

Cannato, Judy. *Quantum Grace: The Sunday Readings: Lenten Reflections on Creation and Connectedness.* Notre Dame, IN: Ave Maria Press, 2003.

Cannato, Judy. *Radical Amazement: Contemplative Lessons from Black Holes, Supernovas, and Other Wonders of the Universe.* Notre Dame, IN: Sorin Books, 2006.

Cannato, Judy. *Field of Compassion: How the New Cosmology is Transforming Spiritual Life.* Notre Dame, IN: Sorin Books, 2010.

Capra, Fritjof. *The Tao of Physics: An Exploration of the Parallels between Modern Physics and Eastern Mysticism*. Boston, MA: Shambhala, 1975.

Capra, Fritjof. *Uncommon Wisdom: Conversations with Remarkable People*. New York: Simon and Schuster, 1988.

Capra, Fritjof. *The Web of Life: A New Scientific Understanding of Living Systems*. New York: Doubleday, 1996.

Capra, Fritjof. *The Hidden Connections: A Science for Sustainable Living*. New York: Doubleday, 2002.

Capra, Fritjof and David Steindl-Rast. *Belonging to the Universe*. San Francisco: Harper, 1991.

Carmelites of Indianapolis. *The Woman's Prayer Companion.* Indianapolis, IN: Carmelite Monastery, 1994.

Cassidy, Laurie and M. Shawn Copeland, eds., *Desire, Darkness, and Hope: Theology in a Time of Impasse*. Collegeville, MN: Liturgical Press Academic, 2021.

Chodron, Pema. *When Things Fall Apart: Heart Advice for Difficult Times*. Boston, MA: Shambhala Classics, 1977.

Chodron, Pema. *Welcoming the Unwelcome: Wholehearted Living in a Brokenhearted World.* Boulder, CO: Shambhala Publications, 2019.

Chopra, Deepak. *The Third Jesus: The Christ We Cannot Ignore*. New York: Harmony Books, 2008.

Christie, Douglas E. *The Blue Sapphire of the Mind: Notes for a Contemplative Ecology*. New York: Oxford University Press, 2013.

The Cloud of Unknowing. Translated by Carmen Acevedo Butcher. Boulder, CO: Shambhala Publications, 2018.

Coelho, Mary Conrow. *Awakening Universe, Emerging Personhood: The Power of Contemplation in an Evolving Universe*. Lima, OH: Wyndham Press, 2002.

Coelho, Mary Conrow. *The Depth of Our Belonging: Mysticism, Physics, and Healing*. Caye Caulker, Belize: Producciones de la Hamaca, 2021.

Cone, James H. *The Cross and the Lynching Tree*. Maryknoll, NY: Orbis Press, 2019.

Conn, Joann Wolski. ed. *Women's Spirituality: Resources for Christian Development*. Mahwah, NJ: Paulist Press, 1986.

Copeland, M. Shawn. *Knowing Christ Crucified: The Witness of African American Religious Experience*. Maryknoll, NY: Orbis Books, 2018.

Cowan, John. *Taking Jesus Seriously: Buddhist Meditation for Christians*. Collegeville, MN: Liturgical Press, 2004.

Crossan, John Dominic. *The Historical Jesus: The Life of a Mediterranean Jewish Peasant*. Edinburgh, Scotland: T. & T. Clark, 1991.

Cunningham, Lawrence S. *Thomas Merton: Spiritual Master, The Essential Writings*. Mahwah, NJ: Paulist Press, 1992.

Deignan, Kathleen, CND, and Libby Osgood, CND, eds. *Teilhard de Chardin A Book Of Hours*. Maryknoll, NY: Orbis Books, 2013.

Delio, Ilia. *Christ in Evolution*. Maryknoll, NY: Orbis Press, 2008.

Delio, Ilia. *The Emergent Christ: Exploring the Meaning of Catholic in an Evolutionary Universe*. Maryknoll, NY: Orbis Press, 2011.

Delio, Ilia. *The Unbearable Wholeness of Being: God, Evolution, and the Power of Love*. Maryknoll, NY: Orbis Press, 2013.

Delio, Ilia. *From Teilhard to Omega: Co-Creating an Unfinished Universe*. Maryknoll NY: Orbis Press, 2014.

Delio, Ilia. *Making All Things New: Catholicity, Cosmology, Consciousness*. Maryknoll, NY: Orbis Press, 2015.

Delio, Ilia. *Love is the Answer. What is the Question?: Selected Writings and Talks 2016 – 2018*. CreateSpace Independent Publishing Platform, 2018.

Delio, Ilia. *The Not-Yet-God: Carl Jung, Teilhard de Chardin, and the Relational Whole*. Maryknoll, NY: Orbis Press, 2023.

De Mello, Anthony. *Sadhana, a Way to God: Christian Exercises in Eastern Form*. New York: Doubleday, 1984.

De Mello, Anthony. *The Song of the Bird*. New York: Doubleday, 1984.

De Mello, Anthony. *One Minute Wisdom*. New York: Doubleday, 1988.

De Mello, Anthony. *Taking Flight: A Book of Story Meditations*. New York: Doubleday, 1988.

Douglas-Klotz, Neil. *Prayers of the Cosmos: Meditations on the Aramaic Words of Jesus*. San Francisco: Harper One, 2009.

Duffy, Kathleen, CSJ. *Teilhard's Mysticism*. Maryknoll, NY: Orbis Press, 2014.

Eckhart, Meister. *Meister Eckhart: Sermons and Treatises*. 3 vols. Edited and translated by M. O'C. Walshe., Shaftesbury, UK: Element Books, 1987.

Edwards, Denis. *Ecology at the Heart of Faith*. Maryknoll, NY: Orbis Press, 2006.

Edwards, Denis. *Deep Incarnation: God's Redemptive Suffering with Creatures*. Maryknoll, NY: Orbis Press, 2019.

Eliot, T.S. *Four Quartets: A Poem*. New York: Harcourt, 1943.

Ellsberg, Robert. *All Saints: Daily Reflections on Saints, Prophets, and Witnesses for Our Time*. New York: Crossroad, 1997.

Ellsberg, Robert and Sr. Wendy Beckett, SNDdeN. *Dearest Sister Wendy: A Surprising Story of Faith and Friendship*. Maryknoll, NY: Orbis Books, 2022.

Emoto, Masaru. *The Hidden Messages in Water*. Hillsboro, OR: Beyond Words Publishing, Inc., 2004.

Falk, Richard. *Religion and Humane Global Governance*. New York: Palgrave, 2001.

Farmer, Ronald L. *Beyond the Impasse, the Promise of a Process Hermeneutic*. Macon, GA: Mercer University Press, 1997.

Finley, James. *The Contemplative Heart*. Notre Dame, IN: Sorin Press, 2000.

FitzGerald, Constance. "A Discipleship of Equals: Voices from Tradition—Teresa of Avila and John of the Cross." In Cassidy and Copeland, *Desire, Darkness, and Hope*. 21-64.

FitzGerald, Constance. "Impasse and the Dark Night." In Cassidy and Copeland, *Desire, Darkness, and Hope.* 77-102.

FitzGerald, Constance. "The Desire for God and the Transformative Power of Contemplation." In Cassidy and Copeland, *Desire, Darkness, and Hope.* 151-172.

FitzGerald, Constance. "Transformation in Wisdom: The Subversive Character and Educative Power of Sophia in Contemplation." In Cassidy and Copeland, *Desire, Darkness, and Hope*. 231-304.

FitzGerald, Constance. "Passion in the Carmelite Tradition: Edith Stein." In Cassidy and Copeland, *Desire, Darkness, and Hope*. 347-372.

FitzGerald, Constance. "Dark Night and the Transformative Influence of Wisdom in John of the Cross." In Cassidy and Copeland, *Desire, Darkness, and Hope*. 409-424.

FitzGerald, Constance. "From Impasse to Prophetic Hope: Crisis of Memory." In Cassidy and Copeland, *Desire, Darkness, and Hope*. 425-453.

Fox, Mathew. *The Coming of the Cosmic Christ*. San Francisco: Harper & Row, 1988.

Fox, Mathew. *Hildegard of Bingen, a Saint for our Times*. Vancouver, Canada: Namaste Publishing, 2013.

Fox, Mathew. *Meister Eckhart, A Mystic Warrior for Our Time*. Novato, CA: New World Library, 2014.

Francis. *Let Us Dream: The Path to a Better Future*. New York: Simon and Schuster, 2020.

Francis. *Laudato Si: On Care for our Common Home.* Encyclical. http://www.vatican.va/content/francesco/en/encyclicals/documents/papa-francesco_20150524_envivlica-laudato-si.html.

Freeman, Laurence. *Jesus the Teacher Within*. UK: Continuum International, 2000.

Fromm, Erich. *The Art of Loving*. New York: Bantam, 1956.

Gebara, Ivone. *Longing for Running Water: Ecofeminism and Liberation*. Minneapolis, MN: Augsburg Fortress, 1999.

Gendlin, Eugene T. *Focusing*. New York: Bantam Books, 2007.

Gilles, Anthony. *People of God: The History of Catholic Christianity.* Cincinnati, OH: St. Anthony Messenger Press, 2000.

Green, Brian. *The Elegant Universe*. New York: W. W. Norton & Company, 2003.

Griffiths, Bede. *A New Vision of Reality: Western Science, Eastern Mysticism and Christian Faith.* Springfield, IL: Templegate Publishers, 1989.

Hafiz. *The Gift: Poems by Hafiz*. Translated by Daniel Ladinsky. New York: Penguin Compass, 1999.

Haight, Roger. *Jesus Symbol of God.* Maryknoll, NY: Orbis Books. 1999.

Haight, Roger. *The Nature of Theology: Challenges, Frameworks, Basic Beliefs*. Maryknoll, NY: Orbis Books, 2022.

Haring, Bernard. *Free and Faithful: My Life in the Catholic Church*. Liguori, MO: Liguori/Triumph, 1989.

Haught, John. *God After Einstein*. New Haven, CT: Yale University Press, 2022.

Haught, John. *A John Haught Reader: Essential Writings on Science and Faith*. Eugene, OR: Wipf and Stock, 2018.

Haught, John. *The New Cosmic Story: Inside Our Awakening Universe.* New Haven, CT: Yale University Press, 2017.

Hawking, Stephen. *The Universe in a Nutshell.* New York: Bantam Books, 2001.

Heyward, Isabel Carter. *The Redemption of God: A Theology of Mutual Relation*. Lanham, MD: The University Press of America, 1982.

Hillman, Anne. *Awakening the Energies of Love: Discovering Fire for the Second Time*. Bramble Books, 2008.

Hinsdale, Mary Ann. *Women Shaping Theology*. Mahway, NJ: Paulist Press, 2004.

Holland, Joseph. *Modern Catholic Social Teaching: The Popes Confront the Industrial Age 1740-1958*. Mahwah, NJ: Paulist Press, 2003.

Houston, Jean. *Godseed: The Journey of Christ*. Wheaton, IL: Quest Books, 1992.

Hubbard, Barbara Marx. *Emergence: The Shift from Ego to Essence*. Charlottesville, VA: Hampton Roads, 2001.

Iain, Matthew. *The Impact of God: Soundings from St. John of the Cross*. London: Hodder & Stoughton, 1995.

Inchausti, Robert. *Thomas Merton's American Prophecy.* Albany, NY: State University of New York Press, 1998.

Isaacs, William. *Dialogue: The Art of Thinking Together.* New York: Currency, 1999.

Jalal al-Din Rumi, *The Essential Rumi*. Translated by Coleman Barks and John Moyne. San Francisco: Harper San Francisco, 1995.

Jaworski, Joseph. *Synchronicity: The Inner Path of Leadership*. San Francisco, CA: Berrett-Koehler Publishers, 1998.

Johnson, Elizabeth A. *Consider Jesus: Waves of Renewal in Christology*. New York: Crossroad, 1994.

Johnson, Elizabeth A. *Truly Our Sister: A Theology of Mary in the Communion of Saints.* New York: Continuum, 2003.

Johnson, Elizabeth A. *Quest for the Living God: Mapping Frontiers in the Theology of God*. New York: Continuum, 2008.

Johnson, Elizabeth A. *Abounding in Kindness: Writing for the People of God.* Maryknoll, NY: Orbis Press, 2015.

Johnson, Elizabeth A. *Ask the Beasts: Darwin and the God of Love.* New York: Bloomsbury Continuum, 2015.

Johnson, Elizabeth A. *She Who Is: The Mystery of God in Feminist Theological Discourse*. New York: Crossroads, 2017.

Johnson, Elizabeth A. *Creation and the Cross: The Mercy of God for a Planet in Peril.* Maryknoll, NY: Orbis Press, 2018.

Johnson, Jeremy. *Seeing Through the World: Jean Gebser and Integral Consciousness*. Seattle, WA: Revelore Press, 2019.

Johnson, Kurt and David Robert Ord. *The Coming Interspiritual Age*. Vancouver, BC: Namaste Publishing, 2012.

Johnston, William. *"Arise, My Love...": Mysticism for a New Era*. Maryknoll, NY: Orbis Press, 2000.

Jones, Chris. *Rise Up!: Broadway and American Society from 'Angels in America' to 'Hamilton.'* New York: Methuen Drama, 2019.

Kaku, Michio. *The Future of the Mind: The Scientific Quest to Understand, Enhance, and Empower the Mind.* New York: Anchor Press, 2014.

Kaufman, Gordon D. *In Face of Mystery: A Constructive Theology.* Cambridge, MA: Harvard University Press, 1993.

Keating, Thomas. *The Human Condition: Contemplation and Transformation.* Mahwah, NJ: Paulist Press, 1999.

Keating, Thomas. *Open Mind, Open Heart: The Contemplative Dimension of the Gospel.* New York: Bloomsbury Continuum, 2006.

Keating, Thomas. *Spirituality, Contemplation and Transformation: Writings on Centering Prayer.* New York: Lantern Press, 2008.

Keating, Thomas. *Reflections on the Unknowable.* Brooklyn, NY: Lantern Books, 2014.

Kernion, Anne Kertz. *Spiritual Practices for the Brain: Caring for Mind, Body and Soul.* Chicago, IL: Loyola Press, 2020.

Keirsey, David and Marilyn Bates. *Please Understand Me: Character and Temperament Types.* Del Mar, CA: Prometheus Nemesis Book Company, 1984.

King, Robert H. *Thomas Merton and Thich Nhat Hanh: Engaged Spirituality in an Age of Globalization.* New York: Continuum, 2001.

King, Karen L. *The Gospel of Mary of Magdala.* Santa Rosa, CA: Polebridge Press, 2003.

King, Ursula. *Spirit of Fire, The Life and Vision of Pierre Teilhard de Chardin.* Maryknoll, NY: Orbis Press, 2015.

King, Ursula. *Christ in All Things: Exploring Spirituality with Pierre Teilhard de Chardin.* Maryknoll, NY: Orbis, 2016.

King, Ursula. *Christian Mystics.* Mahwah, NJ: Hidden Spring, 2001.

Kolbenschlag, Madonna. *Eastward Toward Eve: A Geography of Soul.* New York: Crossroad Publishing, 1996.

Kornfield, Jack. *After the Ecstasy, the Laundry: How the Heart Grows Wise on the Spiritual Path.* London: Rider, 2000.

LaCugna, Catherine Mowry, ed. *Freeing Theology: The Essentials of Theology in Feminist Perspective*. New York: Harper Collins, 1993.

Lachman, Barbara. *The Journal of Hildegard of Bingen: A Novel.* New York: Bell Tower, 1993.

Ladinsky, Daniel. *Love Poems from God: Sacred Voices from the East and West.* New York: Penguin Compass, 2002.

Lanzetta, Beverly. *The Other Side of Nothingness.* Albany, NY: State University of New York Press, 2001.

Lanzetta, Beverly. *Radical Wisdom.* Minneapolis, MN: Fortress Press, 2005.

Lanzetta, Beverly. *Emerging Heart: Global Spirituality and the Sacred.* Minneapolis, MN: Fortress Press, 2007.

Lanzetta, Beverly. *Nine Jewels of Night.* San Diego, CA: Blue Sapphire Books, 2014.

Lanzetta, Beverly. *Path of the Heart.* San Diego, CA: Blue Sapphire Books, 2015.

Laszlo, Ervin. *The Chaos Point: The World at the Crossroads.* Charlottesville, VA: Hampton Roads Publishing, 2006.

Laszlo, Ervin. *WorldShift 2012: Making Green Business, New Politics, and Higher Consciousness Work Together.* Rochester, VT: Inner Traditions, 2009.

Laszlo, Ervin and Allan Combs. *Thomas Berry Dreamer of the Earth: The Spiritual Ecology of the Father of Environmentalism*. Rochester, VT: Inner Traditions, 2011.

Laszlo, Ervin and Jude Currivan. *Cosmos: A Co-Creator's Guide to the Whole-World.* New York: Hay House, 2008.

Leakey, Richard and Roger Lewin. *The Sixth Extinction: Biodiversity and Its Survival.* London: Weidenfeld and Nicholson, 1996.

Leong, Kenneth S. *The Zen Teachings of Jesus*. New York: Crossroad, 1995.

Levy, Paul. *The Quantum Revelation: A Radical Synthesis of Science and Spirituality.* New York: Select Books, 2018.

Liebes, Sidney, Elisabet Sahtouris and Brian Swimme. *A Walk Through Time From Stardust to Us: The Evolution of Life on Earth.* New York: John Wiley & Sons, Inc., 1998.

Lipton, Bruce H. *The Biology of Belief: Unleashing the Power of Consciousness, Matter & Miracles.* Santa Rosa, CA: Mountain of Love, 2005.

Maitri, Sandra. *The Spiritual Dimension of the Enneagram: Nine Faces of the Soul.* New York: Penguin Putnam, 2000.

Maitri, Sandra. *The Enneagram of Passions and Virtues.* New York: Penguin Putnam, 2009.

Macy, Joanna. *World as Lover, World as Self.* Berkeley, CA: Parallax Press, 1991.

Macy, Joanna. *Coming Back to Life.* Stony Creek, CT: New Society Publishers, 1998.

Marion, Jim. *Putting on the Mind of Christ: The Inner Work of Christian Spirituality.* Charlottesville, VA: Hampton Roads, 2011.

Mascetti, Manuela Dunn. *The Song of Eve: Mythology and Symbols of the Goddess.* New York: Simon & Schuster, 1990.

Mascetti, Manuela Dunn. *Christian Mysticism.* New York: Hyperion, 1998.

McEntee, Rory and Adam Bucko. *The New Monasticism, An Interspiritual Manifesto for Contemplative Living.* Maryknoll, NY: Orbis Press, 2015.

McFague, Sally. *The Body of God: An Ecological Theology.* Minneapolis, MN: Augsburg Fortress, 1993.

McFague, Sally. *Super, Natural Christians: How We Should Love Nature.* Minneapolis, MN: Augsburg Fortress, 1997.

McGinn, Bernard. *The Mystical Thought of Meister Eckhart: The Man from Whom God Hid Nothing.* New York: Crossroad, 2001.

McTaggart, Lynne. *The Intention Experiment: Using Your Thoughts to Change Your Life and the World.* New York: Free Press, 2007.

McTaggart, Lynne. *The Field: The Quest for the Secret Force of the Universe.* New York: Harper Perennial, 2002.

Merrill, Nan. *Psalms for Praying: An Invitation to Wholeness.* New York: Continuum International, 2003.

Merton, Thomas. *Contemplative Prayer.* London: Darton, Longman and Todd, 1973.

Merton, Thomas. *The Asian Journal of Thomas Merton.* New York: New Directions Books, 1975.

Merton, Thomas. *The Springs of Contemplation.* New York: Merton Legacy Trust, 1992.

Merton, Thomas. *Thoughts on the East.* New York: New Directions, 1995.

Merton, Thomas. *A Book of Hours.* Edited by Kathleen Deignan, CND. Notre Dame, IN: Sorin Books, 2007.

Merton, Thomas. *The Inner Experience: Notes on Contemplation*. London: SPCK, 2003.

Merton, Thomas. *When the Trees Say Nothing*. Notre Dame, IN: Sorin Books, 2003.

Merton, Thomas. *An Invitation to the Contemplative Life*. Edited by Wayne Simsic. Frederick, MD: The Word Among Us Press, 2006.

Mitchell, Nathan. *Real Presence: The Work of Eucharist*. Chicago, IL: Liturgy Training Publications, 1998.

Moe-Lobeda, Cynthia. *Healing a Broken World: Globalization and God*. Minneapolis, MN: Fortress Press, 2002.

Morley, Janet. *All Desires Known*. Harrisburg, PA: Morehouse Publishing, 1992.

Morwood, Michael. *Is Jesus God?: Finding Our Faith*. New York: Crossroad Publishing Company, 2001.

Morwood, Michael. *Praying a New Story*. Maryknoll, NY: Orbis Books, 2004.

Morwood, Michael. *Prayers for Progressive Christians: A New Template*. Scotts Valley, CA: CreateSpace – Kindle Direct Publishing, 2018.

Newell, John Philip. *Praying with the Earth: A Prayerbook for Peace*. Grand Rapids, MI: William B. Eerdmans, 2011.

Nolan, Albert. *Jesus Today: A Spirituality of Radical Freedom*. Maryknoll, NY: Orbis Press, 2022.

Nouwen, Henri J. M. *The Inner Voice of Love: A Journey through Anguish to Freedom*. New York: Doubleday, 1996.

O'Donohue, John. *Beauty: The Invisible Embrace*. New York: HarperCollins, 2004.

O'Murchu, Diarmuid. *The Meaning and Practice of Faith*. Maryknoll, NY: Orbis Press, 2014.

O'Murchu, Diarmuid. *Adult Faith: Growing in Wisdom and Understanding*. Maryknoll, NY: Orbis Press, 2010.

O'Murchu, Diarmuid. *Catching Up with Jesus: A Gospel Story for Our Time*. New York: Crossroad, 2005.

O'Murchu, Diarmuid. *Evolutionary Faith: Rediscovering God in our Great Story*. Maryknoll, NY: Orbis, 2002.

O'Murchu, Diarmuid. *Religion in Exile: A Spiritual Vision for the Homeward Bound*. New York: Crossroads, 2000.

O'Murchu, Diarmuid. *Poverty, Celibacy, and Obedience*. New York: Crossroad, 1999.

O'Murchu, Diarmuid. *Quantum Theology: Spiritual Implications of the New Physics*. New York: Crossroads Publishing, 1997.

O'Murchu, Diarmuid. *Reclaiming Spirituality: A New Spiritual Framework for Today's World*. Dublin, Ireland: Gill and Macmillan, 1997.

Pagels, Elaine. *Beyond Belief: The Secret Gospel of Thomas*. New York: Random House, 2005.

Palmer, Parker J. *A Hidden Wholeness: The Journey Toward an Undivided Life*. San Francisco: Jossey-Bass, 2004.

Palmer, Parker J. *To Know As We Are Known*. San Francisco: Harper/Collins Publisher, 1983.

Panikkar, Raimon. *Christophany: The Fullness of Man*. Maryknoll, NY: Orbis Press, 2004.

Pearce, Joseph Chilton. *The Death of Religion and the Rebirth of Spirit*. Rochester, VT: Park Street Press, 2007.

Pearce, Joseph Chilton. *The Heart-Mind Matrix: How the Heart Can Teach the Mind New Ways to Think*. Rochester, VT: Park Street Press, 2012.

Pierce, Brian J. *We Walk the Path Together: Learning from Thich Nhat Hanh and Meister Eckhart*. Maryknoll, NY: Orbis, 2005.

Phillips, Jan. *The Art of Original Thinking - The Making of a Thought Leader*. San Diego, CA: 9th Element Press, 2006.

Pramuk, Christopher. *Sophia: The Hidden Christ of Thomas Merton*. Collegeville, MN: Liturgical Press, 2009.

Prevallet, Elaine. *Toward a Spirituality for Global Justice: A Call to Kinship*. Louisville, KY: Sowers Books, 2005.

Primack, Joel R. and Nancy Ellen Abrams. *The View from the Center of the Universe*. New York: Riverhead Press, 2006.

Quinonez, Lora Ann, CDP, and Mary Daniel Turner, SNDdN. *The Transformation of American Catholic Sisters*. Philadelphia, PA: Temple Press, 1992.

Radin, Dean. *Entangled Minds: Extrasensory Experiences in a Quantum Reality*. New York: Paraview Pocket Books, 2006.

Rahner, Karl SJ. *The Mystical Way in Everyday Life*. Edited and translated by Annemarie S. Kidder. Maryknoll, NY: Orbis Books, 2010.

Rainer Maria Rilke. *Rilke's Book of Hours*. Translated by Anita Barrows and Joanna Macy. New York: Riverhead Books, 1996.

Reagan, Michael. *The Hand of God: Thoughts and Images Reflecting the Spirit of the Universe*. Conshohocken, PA: Templeton Press, 2011.

Roberts, Bernadette. *The Path to No Self: Life at the Center*. Albany: State University of New York, 1991.

Rohr, Richard. *Everything Belongs: The Gift of Contemplative Prayer*. New York: Crossroads Publishing, 1999.

Rohr, Richard. *The Universal Christ: How a Forgotten Reality Can Change Everything We See, Hope For, and Believe*. New York: Convergent Books, 2019.

Rohr, Richard and John Bookser Feister. *Hope Against Darkness: The Transforming Vision of Saint Francis in an Age of Anxiety*. Cincinnati, OH: St. Anthony Messenger, 2001.

Rolheiser, Ronald. *The Holy Longing: The Search for a Christian Spirituality*. New York: Doubleday, 1999.

Rolheiser, Ronald. *The Shattered Lantern: Rediscovering a Felt Presence of God*. New York: Crossroad Publishing, 2001.

Roszak, Theodore. *The Voice of the Earth: An Exploration of Ecopsychology*. Grand Rapids, MI: Phanes Press, 1992.

Roszak, Theodore, Mary E. Gomes, and Allen D. Kanner, eds. *Ecopsychology: Restoring the Earth/ Healing the Mind*. San Francisco: Sierra Club, 1995.

Rothluebber, Francis B. *The Upstart Spring: An Experience in Evolutionary Spirituality*. Idyllwild, CA: Colombiere Center, 2005.

Ruether, Rosemary Radford. *Gaia and God: An Ecofeminist Theology of Earth Healing*. San Francisco: Harper, 1992.

Ruffing, Janet K., ed. *Mysticism and Social Transformation*. Syracuse, NY: Syracuse University Press, 2001.

Sardello, Robert. *Silence: The Mystery of Wholeness*. Berkeley, CA: North Atlantic Books, 2006.

Scharmer, C. Otto. *Theory U: Leading from the Future as It Emerges*. Cambridge, MA: Society for Organizational Learning, 2007.

Schenk, Jim, ed. *What Does God Look Like in an Expanding Universe*. Cincinnati, OH: Imago Publishing, 2006.

Schillebeeckx, Edward. *Jesus: An Experiment in Christology*. Translated by Hubert Hoskins. London: Collins, 1979.

Schneiders, Sandra M. *Finding the Treasure: Locating Catholic Religious Life in a New Ecclesial and Cultural Context*. Mahwah, NJ: Paulist Press, 2000.

Schneiders, Sandra M. *With Oil in Their Lamps: Faith, Feminism, and the Future*. Mahwah, NY: Paulist Press, 2000.

Schneiders, Sandra M. *Selling All: Commitment, Consecrated Celibacy, and Community in Catholic Religious Life*. Mahwah, NY: Paulist Press, 2001.

Schneiders, Sandra M. *Buying the Field: Catholic Religious Life in Mission to the World*. Mahwah, NY: Paulist Press, 2013.

Schüssler Fiorenza, Elisabeth. *In Memory of Her: A Feminist Theological Reconstruction of Christian Origins*. New York: Crossroad, 1983.

Schüssler Fiorenza, Elisabeth. *Discipleship of Equals: A Critical Feminist Ekklesialogy of Liberation*. New York: Crossroads Press, 1993.

Senge, Peter. *The Fifth Discipline Fieldbook: Strategies and Tools for Building a Learning Organization*. New York: Doubleday, 1994.

Senge, Peter, C. Otto Scharmer, Joseph Jaworski, and Betty Sue Flowers. *Presence: Human Purpose and the Field of the Future*. New York: Doubleday, 2005.

Sheldrake, Rupert. *The Rebirth of Nature: The Greening of Science and God*. Rochester, VT: Park Street Press, 1994.

Sheldrake, Rupert, Terence McKenna, and Ralph Abraham. *Chaos, Creativity, and Cosmic Consciousness*. Rochester, VT: Park Street Press, 2001.

Smith, Cyprian. *The Way of Paradox: Spiritual Life as Taught by Meister Eckhart*. London: Darton, Longman and Todd, 1987.

Smith, Paul. *Integral Christianity the Spirit's Call to Evolve*. St. Paul, MN: Paragon House, 2001.

Soelle, Dorothee. *The Silent Cry: Mysticism and Resistance*. Minneapolis, MN: Augsburg Fortress, 2001.

Soelle, Dorothee. *Suffering*. Philadelphia, PA: Fortress, 1975.

Soelle, Dorothee. *Revolutionary Patience*. Maryknoll, NY: Orbis Books, 1977.

Spong, John Shelby. *Why Christianity Must Change or Die: A Bishop Speaks to Believers in Exile*. San Francisco: HarperCollins, 1999.

Spong, John Shelby. *A New Christianity for a New World: Why Traditional Faith is Dying and How a New Faith is Being Born.* San Francisco: HarperCollins, 2001.

St. John of the Cross. *Dark Night of the Soul*. Translated by E. Allison Peers. Radford, VA: Wilder, 2008.

St. Teresa of Avila. *Interior Castle*, Edited and translated by E. Allison Peers. Mineola, NY: Dover, 2007.

Steindl-Rast, David. *Gratefulness, the Heart of Prayer: An Approach to Life in Fullness*. Ramsey, NJ: Paulist Press, 1984.

Steindl-Rast, David. *A Listening Heart: The Spirituality of Sacred Sensuousness.* New York: Crossroads Publishing, 1999.

Steindl-Rast, David. *Common Sense Spirituality: The Essential Wisdom of David Steindl-Rast.* Edited by Angela Iadavaia. New York: Crossroad, 2008.

Steindl-Rast, David. *Deeper Than Words: Living the Apostles' Creed*. New York: Image Books, 2010.

Stone, Merlin. *When God Was a Woman*. Boston, MA: Mariner Books/HarperCollins, 1976.

Sussman, Linda. *Speech of the Grail: A Journey Toward Speaking that Heals and Transforms.* New York: Lindisfarne Press, 1995.

Swimme, Brian. *The Hidden Heart of the Cosmos: Humanity and the New Story*. Maryknoll, NY: Orbis, 1996.

Swimme, Brian and Thomas Berry. *The Universe Story: From the Primordial Flaring Forth to the Ecozoic Era: A Celebration of the Unfolding of the Cosmos*. San Francisco: Harper, 1992.

Swimme, Brian and Mary Evelyn Tucker. *Journey of the Universe*. New Haven, CT: Yale University Press, 2011.

Sylvester Nancy and Mary Jo Klick. *Crucible for Change: Engaging Impasse Through Communal Contemplation and Dialogue.* San Antonio, TX: Sor Juana Press, 2004.

Sylvester, Nancy and Maria Riley. *Trouble and Beauty, Women Encounter Catholic Social Teaching*. Washington, DC: Center of Concern, Leadership Conference of Women Religious and Network, 1991.

Taylor, Charles. *Sources of the Self: The Making of Modern Identity.* Cambridge, MA: Harvard University Press, 1989.

Teasdale, Wayne. *A Monk in the World: Cultivating a Spiritual Life.* Novato, CA: New World Library, 2002.

Teilhard de Chardin, Pierre. *How I Believe.* New York: Harper and Row, Perennial Library, 1969.

Teilhard de Chardin, Pierre. *Toward the Future.* Translated by René Hague. New York: Harcourt, 1973.

Tomaino, Charlotte, A. *Awakening the Brain: The Neuropsychology of Grace.* New York: Atria Books, 2012.

Toolan, David. *At Home in the Cosmos.* Maryknoll, NY: Orbis, 2001.

Tracy, David. *On Naming the Present: God, Hermeneutics, and Church.* Maryknoll, NY: Orbis, 1994.

Tucker, Mary Evelyn. *Worldly Wonder: Religions Enter Their Ecological Phase.* Chicago, IL: Open Court, 2003.

Turner, Denys. *The Darkness of God: Negativity in Christian Mysticism.* Cambridge, UK: Cambridge University Press, 1995.

Uhlein, Gabriele. *Meditations with Hildegard of Bingen.* Sante Fe, NM: Bear & CO., 1982.

Underhill, Evelyn. *Mysticism: A Study in the Nature and Development of Spiritual Consciousness.* Mineola, NY: Dover Publications, 2002.

Walker, Alice. *The World Will Follow Joy: Turning Madness Into Flowers.* New York: The New Press, 2013.

Wessels, Cletus. *The Holy Web: Church and the New Universe Story.* Maryknoll, NY: Orbis, 2000.

Wessels, Cletus. *Jesus in the New Universe Story.* Maryknoll, NY: Orbis, 2003.

Wheatley, Margaret J. *Leadership and the New Science: Discovering Order in a Chaotic World.* San Francisco: Berrett-Koehler, 1999.

Wheatley, Margaret J. *Turning to One Another: Simple Conversations to Restore Hope to the Future.* San Francisco: Berrett-Koehler Publishers, 2002.

Wheatley, Margaret J. *Who Do We Choose To Be: Facing Reality, Claiming Leadership, Restoring Sanity.* Oakland, CA: Berrett-Koehler Publishers, 2017.

Wilber, Ken. *A Brief History of Everything.* Boston, MA: Shambhala, 1996.

Wilber, Ken. *The Essential Ken Wilber: An Introductory Reader.* Boston, MA: Shambhala, 1998.

Wilber, Ken. *The Eye of Spirit: An Integral Vision for a World Gone Slightly Mad.* Boston, MA: Shambhala, 2000.

Wilber, Ken. *Integral Psychology: Consciousness, Spirit, Psychology, Therapy.* Boston, MA: Shambhala, 2000.

Wilber, Ken. *The Integral Operating System.* Course on Tape. Sounds True, 2005.

Wilber, Ken. *Integral Spirituality: A Startling New Role for Religion in the Modern and Postmodern World.* Boston, MA: Integral Books, 2006.

Wilber, Ken. *Integral Meditation: Mindfulness as a Way to Grow Up, Wake Up, and Show Up in Your Life.* Boulder, CO: Shambhala, 2016.

Wilber, Ken. *The Religion of Tomorrow: A Vision for the Future of the Great Traditions – More Inclusive, More Comprehensive, More Complete.* Boulder, CO: Shambhala, 2017.

Wiseman, James A. *Spirituality and Mysticism: A Global View.* Maryknoll, NY: Orbis Press, 2006.

Woodhouse, Patrick. *Etty Hillesum: A Life Transformed.* New York: Bloomsbury Academic, 2016.

Woodman, Marion and Jill Mellick. *Coming Home to Myself: Reflections for Nurturing a Woman's Body and Soul.* Berkely, CA: Conari Press, 1998.

Wright, Robert. *The Evolution of God.* New York: Little, Brown, and Company, 2009.

Whyte, David. *Crossing the Unknown Sea: Work as a Pilgrimage of Identity.* New York: Riverhead Books, 2001.

Zohar, Danah. *The Quantum Self.* New York: William Morrow, 1990

Zohar, Danah and Ian Marshall. *The Quantum Society, Mind, Physics, and a New Social Vision.* New York: William Morrow and Company, 1994.

Zohar, Danah and Ian Marshall. *Who's Afraid of Schrodinger's Cat?: The New Science Revealed – Quantum Theory, Relativity, Chaos, and the New Cosmology.* New York: Quill William Morrow, 1997.

Acknowledgements

The entire process of bringing to completion *Journey-Faith in an Entangled World* is one of gratitude. It involved many people who are entangled in my life. I first want to thank my religious community, all the sisters, associates, and elected leaders of the Sisters, Servants of the Immaculate Heart of Mary, Monroe, MI. Their belief in me throughout the years has given me the confidence to continue to follow my heart and my experience of God.

I cannot thank enough the Board of the Institute for Communal Contemplation and Dialogue (ICCD) who provided me the time, space, and courage to bring this book to completion as well as having ICCD serve as publisher. They are Arlene Ashack, IBVM, Susan Schorsten, HM, Jen Disher, and Kathleen Phelan, OP.

Special thanks to the original planning committee in 2001 who brought life into an insight I had and supported me in my awareness of how the various aspects of my journey were intertwined. They were Mary McCann, IHM, Bette Moslander, CSJ, Dorothy Ettling, CCVI, Marcia Allen, CSJ, Nancy Conway, CSJ, Jean Alvarez, and Doris Klein, CSA. Mary Jo Klick was part of the committee and continued to work closely with me shaping the Institute and its programs for close to fifteen years. I also want to thank all those who participated in the various programs of ICCD either as participants or as part of the process teams. Their insights have been extremely valuable.

The increasing clarity of how contemplation is entangled with spiral dynamics integral and evolutionary consciousness came from the intense work I did with Margaret Galiardi, OP first with the focus on the transformative power of communal contemplation and then as we teamed with Vernice Solimar to design and offer *Enter the Chaos: Engage the Differences to Make a Difference*. Some of the women and men who participated in this program meet periodically as alums to discuss how they are integrating their shifting consciousness rooted in contemplation into their lives. Their insights have been invaluable.

Without the invitation by Jan Cebula, OSF, in 2014 to write for the Global Sisters Report (GSR), a part of the *National Catholic Reporter*, I doubt this book would have happened. Writing monthly reflections provided me the opportunity to give voice to how I saw life from a contemplative perspective. It was possible to curate from this vast array of reflections as well as my other writings enough to produce this book. Gail DeGeorge, editor from 2016 untiil September, 2024, was most supportive and encouraging of this project as she read and critiqued some of my earliest attempts to express what I wanted to do with this book.

Although both the text and the bibliography name those people whose writings and insights influenced me, I want to mention two people in particular, Constance FitzGerald, OCD, and Cynthia Bourgeault. Connie and I met periodically starting in 2002 to discuss the various phases of ICCD's first program, Engaging Impasse: Circles of Contemplation and Dialogue. I have kept her informed of what I've been doing and had the privilege of her accompanying me on retreat twice in recent years. Her being and her writings continue to inspire me and give me hope. Cynthia played a significant role as well. When I read her book, *Wisdom Jesus*, I knew she was someone I wanted to get to know. It seemed that we traveled a similar journey of entanglement. Through the years in addition to reading her books, I've participated in a number of her programs in person and online. In 2013 Cynthia accepted an invitation to be part of a program ICCD sponsored, *Exercising Contemplative Power*. Her contemplative heart and genius are amazing.

Lois Dideon, a Cenacle sister, directed my yearly retreat for close to 30 years. Her wisdom and skill in listening to my struggle on the journey allowed me to keep going and confirmed that what I was experiencing truly was Spirit filled.

Of course, the beginning of the journey began in my family who instilled in me the fundamentals of my faith with an emphasis on both being true to one's experience and recognizing that the demands of love might trump the constraints of law. Thank you, Virginia, Joe, Ginny, and Rene. They would be so proud.

Through the years, friends have been a key inspiration for my *Journey-Faith* and have helped me understand the entanglement of my various life experiences. A special thanks to: Carol Coston, OP, Julia Darlow, Elise Garcia, OP, Jane Herb, IHM, Mary Hunt, Barbara Johns, IHM, Karen Hurley Kuchar, KC McBride, Mary Maynard, Diann Neu, KC McKenna Schlee, Pat Siemen, OP, Mary Lynn Sullivan, Kathy Tkach, and IHMs with whom I served in congregational leadership: Paula Cathcart, Anne Crimmins, Mary Ann Markle, Mary McCann, Fran Mlocek, Kate O'Brien, and Mary Agnes Ryan. Writing a book is time consuming and my local IHM community these past years has been very patient and supportive of me in this effort. They even were early readers. I give thanks for Margaret Alandt, Susan Rakoczy, Barbara Stanbridge, and Diane Brown who also helped proof-read and format the bibliography.

I want to thank Rebecca Hodge, OP, ICCD's web designer, who decided in 2022 to compile and print all of my GSR reflections. Seeing them all together like that prompted me to wonder if they could become part of another effort perhaps a book.

I want to thank the early readers who read the evolving manuscript offering excellent insights and encouragement to continue: Arlene Ashack, IBVM, Elizabeth Burns, Jennifer Cartland, Connie FitzGerald, OCD, Margaret Galiardi, OP, Marianne Gaynor, IHM, Jane Herb, IHM, Mary Ann Hinsdale, IHM, Mary Hunt, Katherine Kirkley, Mary Jo Klick, Alan Krema, Karen Hurley Kuchar, Leo Lechtenberg, Marge Polys, IHM, Linda Romey, OSB, BJ Schlachter, and

Erin Zubal, OSU. A special thanks goes to Vernice Solimar, Mary Novak, and Michelle Scheidt who read the manuscript several times as well as those who were willing to read the pre-published manuscript and offered their endorsements found in the front of the book.

Getting a book to publication involves a lot of work and I am very grateful for the time, talent, and expertise of the following women: Linda Delene, and Diane Brown, IHM, copy editors; Rose DeSloover, artistic advisor and illustrator; and Judy Olds, digital image and page designer.

When the book was still an idea, Mary Katherine Hamilton, IHM, graciously offered to read all the GSR reflections and see if they could contribute to a larger effort. Beginning in late 2022, Mary Katherine has been my close collaborator. Our hours talking, writing, rewriting, and wondering all came together in *Journey-Faith in an Entangled World*. Competent, creative, and committed, she persevered from that initial 'yes' to the last decisions regarding publication. She is the curator of my art exhibit, and I am truly grateful.

Finally, a thank you to all those whom I've encountered throughout the years in the various workshops, conferences, programs -- in person and on ZOOM -- or individual conversations whose response to and support of my work helped sustain the energy to make this book a reality. And for all of you whom I've yet to meet who are reading the book, thank-you and may it inspire you to be faithful on your own transformative Journey-Faith in our entangled world.

About the Author

Nancy Sylvester, IHM, founded the Institute for Communal Contemplation and Dialogue in 2002. Prior to that she served in elected leadership positions both within her religious congregation, the Sisters, Servants of the Immaculate Heart of Mary (IHM) of Monroe, MI., and in the Presidency of the Leadership Conference of Women Religious (LCWR). She served on the staff of Network, a D.C. based Catholic Social Justice Lobby, for fifteen years, ten years as Executive Director. Nancy is a well-known speaker, writer, and process facilitator. She has co-authored two books: *Trouble and Beauty, Women Encounter Catholic Social Justice Teaching* and *Crucible for Change*. Her articles have appeared in a variety of publications. She has an undergraduate degree in philosophy and political science from St. Louis University and a master's in human development from St. Mary's University in Winona, MN.

The Institute for Communal Contemplation and Dialogue (ICCD) is a 501c3 organization that fosters and facilitates the larger movement for the transformation of consciousness so as to create new responses to the crises of our time and to cultivate a healthy Earth community. Its unique contribution is its commitment to the transformative power of contemplation. Become part of an ongoing community with periodic mailings, ZOOM calls, and access to a wealth of resources to read on-line or download. Go to our website www.iccdinstitute.org and click join.

Follow us on: Facebook: www.facebook.com/instituteforcommunalcontemplation
　　　　　　　Instagram: www.instagram.com/iccdinstitute/
　　　　　　　X: www.x.com/IccdInstitute
　　　　　　　TikTok: www.tiktok.com/@iccdinstitute

Made in United States
North Haven, CT
24 October 2024